# Welcome to
## Table Talk

C000146487

**Table Talk** helps children and adults explore the Bible together. Each day provides a short family Bible time which, with your own adaptation, could work for ages 4 to 12. It includes optional follow–on material which takes the passage further for older children. There are also suggestions for linking **Table Talk** with **XTB** children's notes.

> **Who can use Table Talk?**

- **Families**
- **One adult with one child**
- **A teenager with a younger brother or sister**
- **Children's leaders with their groups**
- **Any other mix that works for you!**

### Table Talk

A short family Bible time for daily use. Table Talk takes about five minutes, maybe at breakfast, or after an evening meal. Choose whatever time and place suits you best as a family. Table Talk includes a simple discussion starter or activity that leads into a short Bible reading. This is followed by a few questions.

### XTB

**XTB** children's notes help 7-11 year olds to get into the Bible for themselves. They are based on the same Bible passages as **Table Talk**. You will find suggestions for how **XTB** can be used alongside **Table Talk** on the next page.

In the next three pages you'll find suggestions for how to use Table Talk, along with hints and tips for adapting it to your own situation. If you've never done anything like this before, check out our web page for further help (go to www.thegoodbook.co.uk and click on Bible Reading, then Youth, then Table Talk) or write in for a fact sheet.

**THE SMALL PRINT**

Table Talk is published by The Good Book Company, 37 Elm Road, New Malden, Surrey, KT3 3HB
Tel: 0845 225 0880. www.thegoodbook.co.uk   email: alison@thegoodbook.co.uk  Written by Alison Mitchell.
Tasty illustrations by Kirsty McAllister. Bible quotations taken from the Good News Bible.
**AUSTRALIA:** Distributed by Matthias Media. Tel: (02) 9663 1478; email: info@matthiasmedia.com.au

# HOW TO USE
# Table Talk

**Table Talk** is designed to last for up to three months. How you use it depends on what works for you. We have included 65 full days of material in this issue, plus some more low-key suggestions for another 26 days (at the back of the book). We would like to encourage you to work at establishing a pattern of family reading. The first two weeks are the hardest!

**DAY 1**
**What shall we do?**

**KEYPOINT**
When the people heard Peter's speech, they asked, "What shall we do?" **Read Acts 2v38-39**

Today's passages are:
**Table Talk** : Acts 2v38-39
**XTB** : Acts 2v37-40

**TABLE TALK** Recap: Look again at yesterday's five points from Peter's speech.

**READ** When the people heard Peter's speech, they asked, "What shall we do?" **Read Acts 2v38-39**

**TALK** Peter told them to *repent*. What does that mean? (To repent doesn't just mean saying sorry. It means asking God to help you to *change*, and to do what He says.) What two things did Peter say would happen? (Their sins will be forgiven, they'll be given the gift of the Holy Spirit.)

**DO** Use the illustration in **Notes for Parents** (on the previous page) to show how Jesus rescues us from our sins.

**PRAY** Verse 39 means that this promise is for us too—even though we live 2000 years after Peter! Thank God for sending Jesus so that you can be forgiven.

**Building up**
The apostles had the task of telling others about Jesus. Some of them also wrote the books that make up the New T. But what if they *forgot* some of what they had seen or heard? Or didn't *understand* it? **Read John 14v25-26** to see how the Holy Spirit helped them. Thank God for making sure that what the apostles taught and wrote down about Jesus was true and accurate.

**KEYPOINT**
This is the main point you should be trying to convey. Don't read this out—it often gives away the end of the story!

**Table Talk** is based on the same Bible passages as *XTB*, but usually only asks for two or three verses to be read out loud. The full *XTB* passage is listed at the top of each **Table Talk** page. If you are using **Table Talk** with older children, read the full *XTB* passage rather than the shorter version.

The main part of **Table Talk** is designed to be suitable for younger children. ***Building Up*** includes more difficult questions designed for older children, or those with more Bible knowledge.

As far as possible, if your children are old enough to read the Bible verses for themselves, encourage them to find the answers in the passage and to tell you which verse the answer is in. This will help them to get used to handling the Bible for themselves.

The **Building Up** section is optional. It is designed to build on the passage studied in Table Talk (and XTB). Building Up includes some additional questions which reinforce the main teaching point, apply the teaching more directly, or follow up any difficult issues raised by the passage.

## Linking with *XTB*

The **XTB** children's notes are based on the same passages as **Table Talk**. There are a number of ways in which you can link the two together:
- Children do **XTB** on their own. Parents then follow these up later (see suggestions below).
- A child and adult work through **XTB** together.
- A family uses **Table Talk** together at breakfast. Older children then use **XTB** on their own later.
- You use **Table Talk** on its own, with no link to **XTB**.

## FOLLOWING UP XTB

If your child uses **XTB** on their own it can be helpful to ask them later to show you (or tell you) what they've done. Some useful starter questions are:

- Can you tell me what the reading was about?

- Is there anything you didn't understand or want to ask about?

- Did anything surprise you in the reading? Was there anything that would have surprised the people who first saw it or read about it?

- What did you learn about God, Jesus or the Holy Spirit?

- Is there anything you're going to do as a result of reading this passage?

Table Talk is deliberately not too ambitious. Most families find it quite hard to set up a regular pattern of reading the Bible together—and when they do meet, time is often short. So Table Talk is designed to be quick and easy to use, needing little in the way of extra materials, apart from pen and paper now and then.

## BUT!!

Most families have special times when they **can** be more ambitious, or do have some extra time available. Here are some suggestions for how you can use Table Talk as the basis for a special family adventure...

### PICNIC

Take Table Talk with you on a family picnic. Thank God for His beautiful Creation.

### WALK

Go for a walk together. Stop somewhere with a good view and read Genesis 1v1—2v4.

### GETTING TOGETHER

Invite another family for a meal, and to read the Bible together. The children could make a poster based on the passage.

### MUSEUM

Visit a museum to see a display from Bible times. Use it to remind yourselves that the Bible tells us about real people and real history.

### HOLIDAYS

Set aside a special time each day while on holiday. Choose some unusual places to read the Bible together—on the beach, up a mountain, in a boat... Take some photos to put on your Table Talk display when you get back from holiday.

You could try one of the special holiday editions of XTB and Table Talk—**Christmas Unpacked, Easter Unscrambled** and **Summer Signposts.**

# Have an adventure!

### FOOD!

Eat some food linked with the passage you are studying. For example Manna (biscuits made with honey, Exodus 16v31), Unleavened bread or Honeycomb (Matthew 3v4— but don't try the locusts!)

### DISPLAY AREA

We find it easier to remember and understand what we learn when we have something to look at. Make a Table Talk display area, for pictures, Bible verses and prayers. Add to it regularly.

### VIDEO

A wide range of Bible videos are available—from simple cartoon stories, to whole Gospels filmed with real life actors. (Your local Christian bookshop should have a range.) Choose one that ties in with the passages you are reading together. **_Note:_** Use the video **in addition** to the Bible passage, not **instead** of it!

### PRAYER DIARY

As a special project, make a family prayer diary. Use it to keep a note of things you pray for—and the answers God gives you. This can be a tremendous help to children (and parents!) to learn to trust God in prayer as we see how He answers over time.

Go on—try it!

### DRAMA OR PUPPETS

Take time to dramatise a Bible story. Maybe act it out (with costumes if possible) or make some simple puppets to retell the story.

**Enough of the introduction, let's get going...**

## MEET JOHN

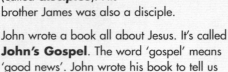

**John** was one of Jesus' closest friends (called *disciples*). His brother James was also a disciple.

John wrote a book all about Jesus. It's called **John's Gospel**. The word 'gospel' means 'good news'. John wrote his book to tell us the good news about *Jesus*.

John also wrote four other Bible books. They are *Revelation*, *1 John*, *2 John* and *3 John*.

## WHO IS THE CHRIST?

Jesus is often called Jesus Christ, but this <u>isn't</u> His surname. He's not called 'Mr Christ'!

**Christ** is a <u>Greek</u> word. The same word in the <u>Hebrew</u> language is **Messiah**. They both mean 'the anointed one'. Being anointed meant having oil poured on your head to make you a king. The names *Christ* and *Messiah* tell us <u>who</u> Jesus is. He is **'God's chosen King'**.

*The picture shows David being anointed with oil by Samuel. This was a sign that David had been chosen by God to be the next king of Israel.*

## SOMETHING TO THINK ABOUT...

In John 20v30, John says that he <u>didn't</u> write down all of Jesus' miracles. Talk about why that might be, and then look up part of John's reason in **John 21v25**.

**KEYPOINT**
John wrote his book so that we may believe that Jesus is the Christ/Messiah.

Today's passages are:
**Table Talk**: John 20v30-31
**XTB**: John 20v30-31

**TABLE TALK**

Welcome to John's Gospel! Ask if your child knows <u>who</u> John was or <u>what</u> he wrote about. Then read 'Meet John' in **Notes for Parents** opposite.

**READ**

When you read a book, you usually start at the <u>beginning</u>. But we're going to start at the <u>end</u>—because that's where John explains why he wrote his book about Jesus... **Read John 20v30-31**

**TALK**

What <u>didn't</u> John include in his book? (v30) (*The other miracles Jesus did.*) But John <u>did</u> include some miracles in his book. Why? (v31) (*So that we may believe that Jesus is the Christ [Messiah] and live with Him for ever in heaven.*)

John is saying that miracles are like **signposts**. They point to <u>who</u> Jesus is, so that we can believe in Him.

**DO**

(*Optional*) **Draw** a large signpost, and write 'Who Jesus is' on it. Put it where you'll all see it as you read John's Gospel.

Find out more about 'the Christ' in **Notes for Parents**.

**PRAY**

Thank God for John's Gospel. Ask Him to help you to learn more about King Jesus as you read John's book, and to believe what you read.

### Building up

Tomorrow, we'll start reading from chapter 4 of John's Gospel. Flick back through chapters 1 to 3 to see what's happened so far. What <u>signs</u> have there been, pointing to who Jesus is? (*eg: John the Baptist calling Jesus 'the lamb of God' in John 1v29, Jesus' first miracle in John 2v1-11...*)

# DAY 2
# Well I never!

**KEYPOINT**
The great news about Jesus is for <u>everyone</u>.

Today's passages are:
**Table Talk:** John 4v1-7
**XTB:** John 4v1-7

**TABLE TALK**

In today's story, Jesus is on His way from **Judea** to **Galilee**. On the way, He stops off in **Sychar**, a town in **Samaria**.

Find all of these places on the map in **Notes for Parents** opposite, and read what it says about the **Samaritans**.

**READ**

We've just seen that <u>Jews</u> didn't talk to <u>Samaritans</u>. **Jesus** was a Jew, but check out what He does... **Read John 4v1-7**

**TALK**

Where did Jesus stop to rest? (v5-6) (*By Jacob's well, outside the town of Sychar.*) What kind of woman did Jesus meet? (v7) (*A Samaritan.*) What did Jesus say to her? (*See v7.*)

**THINK**

Jews didn't talk to <u>Samaritans</u>. But **Jesus** did! Jewish teachers (Rabbis) didn't talk to <u>women</u> either. But **Jesus** did! Why do you think He did that? (*Jesus talked to her about Himself, as we'll see tomorrow. The great news about Jesus is for <u>everyone</u>.*)

**PRAY**

The great news about Jesus is for EVERYONE. It's for Jews, Samaritans, men, women, boys, girls. It's even for people you don't like to talk to! Thank God that the great news about Jesus is for everyone—including **you**!

### Building up

Do you know the story of the Good Samaritan? Jesus told this **parable** (a story with a meaning) to <u>Jewish</u> people. They would have been really shocked when He made a Samaritan the hero of the story! **Read it in Luke 10v25-37**. Jesus' story showed that 'Love your neighbour' meant <u>everyone</u>, not just people we like!

**MEET THE SAMARITANS**
**Sychar** was a city in the area of **Samaria**, which was between **Galilee** and **Judea**. The people living in Samaria were called **Samaritans**.

Jews and Samaritans <u>hated</u> each other. Jews believed that talking to a Samaritan made them unfit for God!

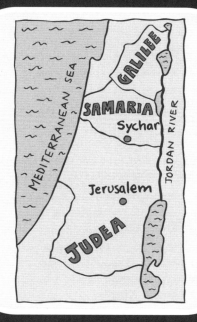

**JACOB'S WELL**
Jacob's well was on land that had been bought by Jacob 2000 years earlier (*Genesis 33v18-19, Joshua 24v32*). In a hot country, without plumbing, wells were a vital source of water. The Samaritan woman would have come there every day to draw fresh water from the well.

# DAY 3
# Living water

**KEYPOINT**
Jesus gives eternal life to everyone who believes and trusts in Him.

Today's passages are:
**Table Talk:** John 4v7-14
**XTB:** John 4v7-14

**TABLE TALK**

Put a glass of water on the table. Where did it come from? (*eg: a tap, from the mains, from a water purification plant...*) People didn't have taps in Bible times, so their water came from <u>rivers</u> or a <u>well</u> (like the one in yesterday's story).

**Recap:** Who did Jesus talk to? (*A Samaritan woman.*) Why was that surprising? (*Jews didn't talk to Samaritans, and Jewish teachers didn't talk to women.*)

**READ**

Jesus really surprised the Samaritan woman by talking to her...
**Read John 4v7-14**

**TALK**

Jesus spoke about **water**, but <u>not</u> the kind that comes from a well. What kind of water was Jesus talking about? (v10) (*Living water/Life-giving water*) Why was the woman puzzled? (v11) (*Jesus didn't have a bucket to get water from the well.*) But Jesus wasn't talking about water to <u>drink</u>. What would 'living water' give someone? (v14) (*Eternal life*)

**THINK**

**Wow!** Jesus was offering this woman eternal life! Eternal life isn't just life for ever. It's knowing Jesus as our Friend and King <u>now</u> so that one day we will live with Him for ever. It's for everyone who believes and trusts in **Him**—the only One who can give it.

**PRAY**

If you are a Christian (a follower of Jesus) then you already have His fantastic gift of eternal life. Thank Him for it now.

## Building up
The most famous verse in the Bible is also about eternal life. Check it out in **John 3v16**.

---

# DAY 4
# Who is Jesus?

**KEYPOINT**
Jesus is God's chosen King (the Christ/Messiah) who came to rescue us.

Today's passages are:
**Table Talk:** John 4v15-18 & 25-26
**XTB:** John 4v15-26

**TABLE TALK**

What kind of water has Jesus offered the Samaritan woman? (*Living water.*) What did He mean? (*Eternal life.*)

**READ**

The Samaritan woman thinks Jesus is offering her water that will stop her getting thirsty... **Read John 4v15-18**

**TALK**

This woman had never met Jesus before, but He knew all about her! What did Jesus know? (*She'd had five husbands, and was now living with another man.*)

**READ**

The woman thought Jesus was a <u>prophet</u> (a messenger from God) so she asked Him a religious question about <u>where</u> God should be worshipped. (See Building Up if you want to read about this.) But Jesus had something far more important to tell her... **Read John 4v25-26**

**TALK**

Who did Jesus say He was? (v26) (*The Messiah/Christ.*) Wow! This Samaritan woman had just found out that Jesus is the Messiah (Christ). He is God's chosen King, who came to rescue us!

**THINK**

Jesus, God's chosen King, knew this woman wasn't living as God wanted. Disaster! Except that He had come to rescue her from her sin. Fantastic!

**PRAY**

What wrong stuff does King Jesus know about you? Thank God for sending Him to rescue you from all that.

## Building up
**Read John 4v19-24.** Jews and Samaritans didn't agree about <u>where</u> God should be worshipped. But Jesus had something far more important to tell the woman. What did He say about 'salvation'? (*Salvation is from the Jews, v22.*) Salvation means 'rescue from sin'. Jesus was a <u>Jew</u>. He came to <u>rescue</u> us from sin.

# DAY 5
## Tell tale

KEYPOINT
The Samaritan woman told others about Jesus, and invited them to meet Him.

Today's passages are:
**Table Talk**: John 4v27-30
**XTB**: John 4v27-30

**TABLE TALK**
Tell each other some **news**—it might be about someone you've met this week, or something you're planning to do today or... In today's story, someone has some exciting news to tell.

**READ**
While Jesus has been talking to the Samaritan woman, His disciples have been off buying food. Now they're back with lunch, and about to get a shock... **Read John 4v27-30**

**TALK**
Why were the disciples surprised? (v27) (*Jesus was talking to a woman, which Jewish teachers didn't do.*) Where did the woman go? (v28-29) (*Back to town.*) What did she say to the people? (v29) (*'Come and see a man who told me everything I ever did. Could he be the Messiah/Christ?'*)

The woman dashed back to town to tell them about Jesus. She didn't know much about Jesus yet—but she told them what she knew, and invited them to come and meet Him.

**THINK**
This woman is a great example for us to follow! Maybe you feel you don't know much about Jesus. Don't worry! Just tell your friends what you do know, and invite them to find out more. Think of a friend or family you could tell about Jesus (and maybe invite to come to church with you). Now ask God to give you a chance to do it!

**PRAY**

### Building up
All Christians are to be ready to tell others about Jesus whenever they can. **Read 1 Peter 3v15**. What might you say if a friend asks why you're a Christian?

# DAY 6
## Harvest time

KEYPOINT
Jesus' 'food' was to obey His Father, God.

Today's passages are:
**Table Talk**: John 4v31-38
**XTB**: John 4v31-38

**TABLE TALK**
Each collect one thing from the kitchen that you love to eat. Now tell the others why you like it.

**READ**
In today's verses we read about Jesus' favourite food—but it's not the kind of food you eat! **Read John 4v31-34**

**TALK**
What did Jesus say His food is? (v34) (*'To do the will of him who sent me and to finish his work.'*) Who does Jesus mean when He talks about 'him who sent me'? (*God, His Father.*)

Jesus is saying that His top task is to obey His Father, God.

**THINK**
Jesus goes on to say that this means telling people about Himself, and these people becoming Christians (v35-38, see Building Up below). That's what Jesus was doing when He talked to the Samaritan woman. You can see why chatting to her was loads more important than munching His lunch!

**PRAY**
Who did you pray for at the end of yesterday's Table Talk? Have you told them about Jesus yet? If you have, that's great! Thank God for helping you to do it. If you haven't, don't worry—but don't leave it either! Plan a time to talk to them, then ask God to help you.

### Building up
**Read John 4v35-38**. These verses are a bit tricky! Jesus is talking about the harvest of eternal life. That means telling people about Jesus. And those people becoming Christians. Pray for people you know who aren't Christians. Ask God to use you as His harvest workers.

# DAY 7
## Check it out

Today's passages are:
**Table Talk**: John 4v39-42
**XTB**: John 4v39-42

 **TABLE TALK**
Imagine if someone phones to tell you there's a giraffe walking down the high street. What would you do? (Go and see for yourself? Ring the zoo? Assume it's not true, and do nothing?)

 **READ**
The Samaritan woman had told the people from her town all about Jesus. It was **amazing news**—so the people went to check it out for themselves...
**Read John 4v39-42**

 **TALK**
What did the people beg Jesus to do? (v40) (*Stay with them.*) How long did Jesus stay? (v40) (*Two days.*) This meant the Samaritans could hear Jesus for themselves. What did they believe about Him now? (v42) (*He's the Saviour of the world.*)

 **THINK**
The Samaritans checked out what they'd been told about Jesus. <u>We</u> should do the same. When you hear a talk in church or a Christian group, or read something in Table Talk, how can you know if it's true? (*Check it out for yourself in the Bible.*)

> Dear Table Talk Readers,
> When I write Table Talk, I try very hard to only write things that are true. But I'm not perfect, and I might make mistakes! So please always check what I've written. Look up the Bible verses, and see for yourselves what they say. Check that I've got it right.
> Thanks! Alison

 **PRAY**
Pray for the people who teach you the Bible. Ask God to help them to teach it correctly, and ask Him to help you to check it out for yourselves.

### Building up
In Acts we read about another group who rightly checked what they being taught. **Read Acts 17v10-12**.

---

# DAY 8
## One o'clock miracle

Today's passages are:
**Table Talk**: John 4v49-54
**XTB**: John 4v46-54

 **TABLE TALK**
Talk about a time when your child was ill. How did <u>they</u> feel? How did <u>you</u> feel?

 **READ**
In today's story, a boy is ill. His dad is very worried, and has walked 20 miles to see Jesus. He finds Jesus at one o'clock in the afternoon ('the seventh hour' in Jewish time-keeping.) But Jesus doesn't come with him! **Read John 4v49-50**

 **TALK**
What did Jesus tell the man to do? (v50) (*Go home.*)

Imagine the man walking 20 miles home again. It would take all night! How do you think he felt as he hurried home to see his son? (*Hopeful? Worried? Trusting? Scared?*)

 **READ**
The next day, when the man was nearly home, his servants rushed out to meet him. **Read John 4v51-54**

 **TALK**
What time had the boy got better? (v52) (*One o'clock—at the time Jesus was talking to his dad!*) How did the man and his family react? (v53) (*They believed in Jesus.*)

 **THINK**
**Read v50 again**. The father didn't wait for proof. He took Jesus at His word. That's what **faith** is. Faith isn't a feeling. It means <u>believing</u> that what God says in the Bible is true.

**PRAY**
Faith is a gift from God. If <u>you</u> believe God's words in the Bible, thank God for helping you to believe. If you're not sure, ask God to give you the gift of faith.

### Building up
This was Jesus' <u>second</u> miraculous sign (v54). Read about His <u>first</u> one in **John 2v1-11**.

# DAY 9
# Mat matters

**TABLE TALK**

Do you know anyone who uses a wheelchair? What things can't you do if you can't use your legs? What would you miss most?

**READ**

There was a pool in Jerusalem where ill people waited every day. They believed the water could cure them—but **only** if it started to bubble—and **only** the first person to get in! One day Jesus went there and spoke to a man who hadn't been able to walk for a very l-o-n-g time... **Read John 5v1-6**

*The pool looked like this.*

**TALK**

How long had the man been ill? (v5) (*38 years!*) What did Jesus ask the man? (v6) (*'Do you want to get well?'*) What do you think the man might have said? <u>Think</u> about it first, and then <u>read</u> his answer in **John 5v7-9**

The man gave a very grumbly answer, didn't he! Did Jesus still heal him? (v9) (*Yes!*)

**THINK**

This man couldn't make <u>himself</u> better. He couldn't even get himself into the pool! Who was the <u>only</u> person who could heal him? Did you say Jesus? Or God? Both are right! Why? (*Because Jesus <u>is</u> God*)

**PRAY**

This miracle was another signpost pointing to <u>who</u> Jesus is. Only God could heal this man—but Jesus **is** God! So... Do you trust Him? ...listen to Him? ...obey Him? ...love Him? Talk to Him about these things now.

## Building up
Telling this man to get up may have sounded silly, but he obeyed Jesus (v8-9), and was healed. Do you ever <u>disobey</u> Jesus because it seems silly or hard?

# DAY 10
# Missing the point

**TABLE TALK**

(*You need pencil and paper.*) Jesus had just healed a man who had been ill for 38 years! How do you think the man felt? ***Draw his face.***

This all happened on the **Sabbath**, God's special day of rest. But the Jewish leaders had made extra hard rules about the Sabbath. One rule was that you mustn't carry anything!

**READ**

Some of the Jewish leaders saw the man who had been healed...
**Read John 5v10-16**

**TALK**

What did the Jewish leaders say? (v10) (*Stop carrying your mat! It's against the rules!*) The religious leaders should have been <u>thrilled</u> that this man was better. But instead, they were <u>cross</u> because he was carrying a mat! ***Draw their faces.***

**THINK**

Yesterday, we saw that this miracle was like a **signpost**. What did it show? (*That Jesus is God.*) But the Jewish leaders missed the point. What did they decide to do? (v16) (*Persecute Jesus [give Him a hard time] because He broke their Sabbath rules.*)

**PRAY**

The Jewish leaders **missed the point** about Jesus. As you read John's Gospel, ask God to help you to understand what you read about Jesus, so that you don't miss the point about who Jesus is and how to follow Him.

## Building up
Sadly, many Jewish people were like these leaders and refused to believe that Jesus was the Messiah (the promised King) they had been waiting for. The very beginning of John's book says that they would react like this: read **John 1v10-13**. But what's the great promise for those who <u>believe</u> in Jesus? (John 1v12)

# DAY 11
## My Father is...

**KEYPOINT**
The Jewish leaders refused to believe that Jesus was God's Son.

Today's passages are:
**Table Talk:** John 5v17-18
**XTB:** John 5v17-18

**TABLE TALK**

**Recap:** Jesus met a man who had been ill for 38 years. What did Jesus do? (*Heal him.*) What day was it? (*The Sabbath*) How did the Jewish leaders react? (*They were cross because the man was carrying his mat on the Sabbath!*)

**READ**

Those Jewish leaders completely missed the point about who Jesus is—so Jesus made it extra clear to them...
**Read John 5v17-18**

**TALK**

What did Jesus say? (v17) (*'My Father is always working, and I too must work.'*) Who does Jesus mean by 'my Father'? (*God*)

God works all the time, including on the Sabbath. Jesus is saying that He is God's Son, and does the same work that His Father does. That's fantastic! But the Jewish leaders didn't think so. What did they decide to do? (v18) (*Kill Jesus*)

**THINK**

When the Jewish leaders heard Jesus say that God was His Father, they refused to believe it. What do you think? (*That it might be true and you'd like to find out more? That it is true? That you'd like to tell your friends about Jesus?*) Talk about your answers, and then pray together about it. If you need God's help, ask Him for it.

**PRAY**

### Building up
The Bible teaches that there is one God, made of three persons—the Father, the Son (Jesus) and the Holy Spirit. This is called the Trinity. All three persons of the Trinity can be seen at Jesus' baptism—read **Mark 1v9-11.**

---

# DAY 12
## Honour Jesus

**KEYPOINT**
Jesus is the most important person in the world. We must honour Him.

Today's passages are:
**Table Talk**: John 5v19-23
**XTB**: John 5v19-23

**TABLE TALK**

(*You need pen and paper.*) As a Scot, I did lots of Scottish country dancing at school. Every dance started with the command: 'Honour your partner', which means to bow or curtsy to them. Take it in turns to see who can do the most flourishing bow or curtsy.

**READ**

Today's verses say we must **honour** Jesus. But that doesn't mean bowing to Him! **Read John 5v19-23**

**TALK**

These verses are quite tricky! Copy these four sentences onto some paper, then fill in the verse that matches each sentence:

• Jesus does what **God** does (v ____)

• God shows Jesus His **plans** (v ____)

• Jesus has power to give **life** (v ____)

• God gives Jesus the right to **judge** (v ___

(*The answers are v19, v20, v21, v22.*)

**DO**

**Wow!** These verses say that Jesus is the most important person in the world! What does v23 say we must do? (*Honour Jesus, the Son.*) Write 'HONOUR JESUS' at the bottom of your paper. Put it where you'll all see it this week.

**THINK**

To **honour Jesus** means to show Him love and respect. How will you honour Him this week? (*eg: tell Him how great He is, live in a way that pleases Him, tell others about Him...*)

**PRAY**

Ask God to help you do these things.

### Building up
One day everyone will honour Jesus! **Read Philippians 2v9-11.**

# Jesus our judge

**KEYPOINT**
Jesus is both our Judge and our Rescuer.

Today's passages are:
**Table Talk**: John 5v24
**XTB**: John 5v24-30

**TABLE TALK**

Ask your child to think of times or places where there is a **judge**—and talk about what the judge does. (eg: at a dog show, a gymnastics competition, a law court...)

**READ**

At a <u>dog show</u>, the judge chooses the best dog. There's a prize for winning, but it's not too important. In <u>court</u>, the judge decides what punishment to give. Someone may go to prison, or be set free. That's pretty important! But when **Jesus** judges us, He decides if we live <u>with</u> Him for ever in heaven, or <u>without</u> Him for ever. That's totally important!!! **Read John 5v24**

**TALK**

Who does Jesus say will have eternal life? (*Whoever hears Jesus' words and believes Him who sent Jesus.*)

**DO**

Yesterday, we saw that God gives Jesus the right to be our <u>Judge</u>. Use **Notes for Parents** opposite to see how Jesus is our **Judge**, and also our **Rescuer**.

**PRAY**

Thank God for sending Jesus to rescue you.

**WANT TO KNOW MORE?**
For a free booklet called **Why did Jesus die?** write to Table Talk, 37 Elm Road, New Malden, Surrey, KT3 3HB

Or email me at: alison@thegoodbook.co.uk

## Building up
Read the rest of Jesus' words in **John 5v25-30**. These verses are tricky, but notice that **God** gives Jesus the right to be Judge (v27) and that Jesus' judgement is always **right** (v30).

# Notes for Parents

**JESUS IS OUR JUDGE AND RESCUER**
(You need pencil and paper.) *Draw a person (a stick man is fine) on the paper.*

God has given Jesus the right to be our **Judge**. But there's a problem! We are all <u>guilty</u> (have to be punished)—because we all <u>sin</u>.

**ASK: What is sin?**
Sin is more than just doing wrong things. We all like to be **in charge** of our own lives. We do what **we** want instead of what **God** wants. This is called sin.

Because we all sin, we are all guilty, and deserve to be punished.

*Write GUILTY on your picture.*

GUILTY

**ASK: What does sin do?**
Sin gets in the way between us and God. It stops us from knowing God and from being His friends.

But the great news is that Jesus came to rescue us from our sins! If we <u>believe</u> in Jesus, and come to Him to be forgiven, we will still be judged, but we will be found Not Guilty and won't be punished!

*Add NOT to your picture.*

NOT GUILTY

**ASK: Why will we be found "Not Guilty"?**
When Jesus died on the cross He was being punished. He took the punishment that we deserve, so that we can be forgiven. He was found Guilty, so that we can be found Not Guilty.

If we believe in Jesus there is nothing to get in the way between us and God any more. Nothing to stop us knowing Him and being His friends. Jesus has <u>rescued</u> us from our sin.

# DAY 14
## The witnesses

**KEYPOINT**
Jesus' miracles, and the Old Testament promises, showed that Jesus came from God.

Today's passages are:
**Table Talk**: John 5v36-40
**XTB**: John 5v31-40

**TABLE TALK**

Write these letters on eight pieces of paper: **A,D,E,G,O,S,S,V**. Hide them round the room for your child to find. Ask them to arrange the letters to spell 'GOD SAVES'.

The name **Jesus** means 'God saves'. It tells us <u>who</u> Jesus is (He is **God**) and <u>what</u> Jesus does (He **saves** us from our sins).

**READ**

In the last few days we've seen that Jesus is **God** (Day 9) and that He came to **save** us (Day 13). But the Jewish leaders didn't believe it—so Jesus told them about the <u>witnesses</u>... **Read John 5v36-40**

**TALK**

Do you remember what Jesus' <u>miracles</u> are like? (*Signposts, Day 1.*) What do the amazing things Jesus did show about Him? (v36) (*He was sent by God.*) What did the Jewish leaders study? (v39) (*The Scriptures ie: the Old Testament.*) The Old T is full of promises about <u>Jesus</u>—but the Jewish leaders hadn't spotted them! (*We'll see some examples tomorrow...*)

**PRAY**

Getting stuck into the Bible is the best way to learn more about Jesus. But you don't want to be like those Jewish leaders!—so ask God to help you understand and believe what you read.

### Building up
Jesus' miracles, and the Old T Promises, were witnesses to <u>who</u> Jesus is. The other witness was a person: **read John 5v31-35**. Who is Jesus talking about? (v33) (*John the Baptist*) Flick back to **John 1v29** to see what John said about Jesus.

---

# DAY 15
## Moses supposes

**KEYPOINT**
Moses wrote about Jesus—but the Jewish leaders refused to believe in Jesus.

Today's passages are:
**Table Talk**: John 5v45-47
**XTB**: John 5v41-47

**TABLE TALK**

**Quick Quiz:** Are these four facts about Moses true or false?
**a)** The names Moses means 'saved from the water'.
**b)** Moses had a brother called Airy.
**c)** Moses led the Israelites out of Egypt.
**d)** Moses wrote the last five books of the Old Testament.
(*Answers:* **a**—T, **b**—F, he was called Aaron, **c**—T, **d**—F, he wrote the <u>first</u> five books of the Old T.)

**READ**

The Jewish leaders were big fans of Moses. He wrote the first five books of the Old T, and they knew those books back to front! But Jesus told them off, because they didn't <u>believe</u> what Moses had written... **Read John 5v45-47**

**TALK**

Who did Moses write about? (v46) (*Jesus*) Did the Jewish leaders believe in Jesus? (v46-47) (*No!*) So Jesus told them that they didn't believe Moses!

**DO**

(*Optional*) Check out something that Moses wrote about Jesus in <u>Deuteronomy 18v15</u>. God promised that He would send a prophet (God's messenger) like Moses. This new prophet was **Jesus**!

**PRAY**

We'll come back to John's Gospel on Day 41. But for now, think back over the things you've learnt about Jesus in chapters 4 and 5. (Flick back through the headings in your Bible.) What do you want to thank Jesus for?

### Building up
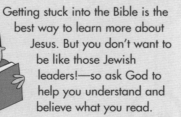
Check out another of Moses' writings in **Genesis 49v10**. A <u>sceptre</u> is a pole carried by a king. This verse says that someone from Judah's family would be king for ever. That king is **Jesus**!

### THE BOOK OF 1 KINGS

The book of **1 Kings** is all about the <u>kings</u> of Israel. So is the book that comes after it, called **2 Kings**.

These books tell us about the kings who came after King David. There was a gaggle of good kings, and a bunch of bad kings!

### Good Kings

- Loved and obeyed God.
- Listened to God's messengers, the prophets.
- Helped their people to live for God.

### Bad Kings

- Disobeyed God.
- Ignored the prophets.
- Prayed to pretend gods (statues), and led their people to pray to pretend gods too.

King David    King Solomon

**KEYPOINT**
David told his son Solomon how to be a good king—by 'walking in God's ways'.

Today's passages are:
**Table Talk:** 1 Kings 2v1-4
**XTB:** 1 Kings 2v1-4

**TABLE TALK**

Welcome to the book of 1 Kings! What do you think it's about? (*Ask your child, then read <u>Notes for Parents</u> together.*)

**READ**

The books just before 1 Kings are 1 and 2 Samuel, where we read about King **David**. David had been a <u>good</u> king. Before he died, David told his son **Solomon** how <u>he</u> could be a good king too... **Read 1 Kings 2v1-4**

**TALK**

What did David tell Solomon to do? (v3) (*Obey God's laws/Walk in His ways.*) Many Bible versions use the words 'Walk in His ways' in verse 3. This means to <u>love</u> God and <u>obey</u> His laws. If Solomon, and the kings who came after him, walked in God's ways, what promise would God keep? (v4) (*That someone from David's family would always be king of Israel.*)

**THINK**

I'm not a king or queen—and I guess you're not either! But God still calls us to **walk in His ways**. Talk about what that might mean for you. (*Eg: reading the Bible, praying, always telling the truth, not fighting with your brother or sister, not gossiping...*)

**PRAY**

What makes it hard for you to obey God? If you want to walk in God's ways, tell Him the things you find hard, and then ask Him to help you. He will!

### Building up
The Old T tells us about someone else who 'walked in God's ways'—so much so, that God took him to be with Him in heaven! **Read Genesis 5v21-24**.

# DAY 17
# Solomon's choice

 **TABLE TALK**

Have you ever read a story where someone is given three wishes? (*Talk about examples.*)

 **READ**

Today's true story from the Bible is a bit like that—except it's REAL! The wonderful God of the universe really did offer to give Solomon anything he wanted! **Read 1 Kings 3v5**

 **THINK**

*Wow!* What an amazing offer! What would you ask for?

Now read Solomon's answer. **Read 1 Kings 5v6-15**

 **TALK**

Solomon knew how hard it would be to rule God's people well. So what did he ask for? (v9) (*Wisdom to rule God's people and to know the difference between right and wrong.*) How did God feel about Solomon's answer? (v10) (*God was pleased.*) Did God give Solomon the wisdom he asked for? (v12) (*Yes*) What else did God give Solomon? (v13) (*Riches and honour.*)

 **PRAY**

*Wow!* Look how generous God is! Not only did He give Solomon more wisdom than anyone had ever had, but He gave him riches and honour as well! When you are praying, this is the wonderful generous God you are praying to. Pray to Him now and thank Him for His generosity.

## Building up
God is wonderfully generous, which is most clearly seen by His gift of His own Son, who came to rescue us. **Read Romans 8v28-32**.

# DAY 18
# How to pray

 **TABLE TALK**

(*You need pen and paper.*) Jot down some of the things you can remember praying about recently. Do you know what God's answers are yet?

 **READ**

Sometimes praying feels **easy**—when there's something exciting to thank God for, or we have a particular problem we need His help with. But sometimes praying is really **hard**, and we can't think what to say! Read Solomon's prayer again from yesterday's story. **Read 1 Kings 3v6-9**

This prayer gives us a great pattern to follow:

 **TALK**

**1** Thanking God for His kindness.

Solomon thanked God for being so kind to His father David (v6) Write down some things you can thank God for.

**2** Praising God for keeping His promises.

The Israelites had become 'a great people, too many to count or number' (v8). This is what God had promised Abraham 1000 years earlier. Write down a promise you want to praise God for.

**3** Praying for the good of God's people.

Solomon knew the Israelites needed a good king, who would rule them wisely. He asked for wisdom for their sake, rather than his own (v9). Think of some of God's people today (eg: Christians you know). What do you want to pray for them?

 **PRAY**

Now use what you've written down to pray in these three ways.

## Building up
Jesus' disciples asked Him to teach them how to pray. Read His answer in **Luke 11v1-4**. Do you know what this prayer is called? (*The Lord's Prayer*) Say it together now.

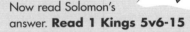

# Notes for Parents

# One baby—two mums!

## ONE BABY—TWO MUMS!

Two women, who lived in the same house, both had babies.

During the night, one of the babies died.

But the woman whose baby died swapped her dead baby for the living one!

In the morning, when the other woman woke up, she found a dead baby beside her.

But it wasn't _her_ baby!

The women argued about it—so they went to see Solomon.

The living baby is mine! No—it's mine!

Solomon found a wise way to settle their argument.
Bring me a sword.

Now cut the living child in half, and give half to each woman.

Based on 1 Kings 3v16-25

---

### KEYPOINT
Solomon's wise ruling showed that God had given him wisdom. But the <u>wisest</u> Ruler is Jesus.

Today's passages are:
**Table Talk:** 1 Kings 3v24-28
**XTB:** 1 Kings 3v16-28

**TABLE TALK**

**Recap:** What gift had Solomon asked God for? (_Wisdom_) Now it was time to use it! Read the cartoon story in **Notes for Parents**.

**READ**

What a shocking thing for Solomon to suggest! Read the passage to see what happened. **Read 1 Kings 3v24-28**

**TALK**

How did Solomon work out who the real mum was? (v27) (_She was the one who wouldn't allow her child to be killed._) How did the Israelites react when they heard about this? (v28) (_They were filled with deep respect for Solomon._)

**THINK**

Solomon had more wisdom than anyone else, but even so, Solomon was nothing like as wise or good as the 'King of Kings'. Look carefully at the cartoon story and you'll see a <u>letter</u> hidden in each picture. If you copy the letters, in order, what name do they spell?

— — — — — — —

**PRAY**

King Jesus is our perfect, wise Ruler. He always does and says what's right. He always knows the best way for us to live, and will show us if we ask Him. Ask King Jesus to show you, through the Bible, the wisest way to live. And if anything is worrying you, ask Jesus to show you the wise answer to it.

### Building up
Jesus' enemies tried to trap Him with trick questions, but He was far too wise to be caught by them! **Read Luke 20v19-26**. <u>Note:</u> Jesus <u>was</u> eventually handed over to the authorities—but the timing was in <u>His</u> hands, not His enemies. King Jesus was always in control!

# DAY 20
## Lots and lots

**KEYPOINT**
God kept His promise to give Abraham a HUGE family. His family were the Israelites.

Today's passages are:
**Table Talk**: 1 Kings 4v20 & Gen 22v17
**XTB**: 1 Kings 4v1-20

**TABLE TALK**
Do you know anyone with an unusual or really l-o-n-g name?

**DO**
**1 Kings 4v1-19** lists <u>lots</u> of people. They have great names like **Zadok**, **Ben-Deker** or **Jehoshaphat**! Scan the lists and choose your favourite names.

Solomon ruled wisely, just as God said he would. These men helped Solomon to do it.

**READ**
In verse 20 there's <u>lots</u> of something else as well... **Read 1 Kings 4v20**

What were there lots of? (v20) (*The 'people of Judah and Israel', which means all of the Israelites.*)

1000 years earlier, God had made a promise to **Abraham**. Read God's promise in **Genesis 22v17**.

**TALK**
What did God promise Abraham? (*That his family [the Israelites] would become too HUGE to count.*) Did God keep that promise? (*Yes*)

**PRAY**
God <u>always</u> keeps His promises. Thank God that nothing (and no one!) can stop His words coming true.

### Building up
God promised Abraham something else as well: **read Genesis 22v18**. God said that someone from Abraham's family would be God's way of blessing the whole world. How did God keep that promise? (*By sending His Son Jesus, who died for us so that our sins can be forgiven.*)

# DAY 21
## The promise keeper

**KEYPOINT**
God is the Promise Keeper. He kept all of His promises to Abraham and David.

Today's passages are:
**Table Talk**: 1 Kings 4v21-25
**XTB**: 1 Kings 4v21-28

**TABLE TALK**
(*You need pen and paper.*) Write 'God's Promises' at the top, then write: **'1—A huge family'**. Yesterday we saw that God had promised to give someone a huge family. Who was that? (*Abraham*) Now we're going to find out about two more promises:

**DO**
Write: **'2—Land'**. God promised to give Abraham's family (the Israelites) all of the land from the border of Egypt to the great river Euphrates. (*This promise is in Genesis 15v18.*)

Write: **'3—Peace'**. God promised David that the Israelites would have peace from their enemies. (*This promise is in 2 Samuel 7v10-11.*)

**READ**
Now read today's verses (about Solomon's rule as king) and look out for clues that these two promises had come true. **Read 1 Kings 4v21-25**

**TALK**
Which verses show that the Israelites were living in the **land** God promised them? (*Answer—v21&v24.*) Which verses show that the Israelites had the **peace** God had promised them? (*Answer—v24&v25.*)

**THINK**
Our wonderful God <u>makes</u> and <u>keeps</u> promises to His people. Do you have a favourite promise from the Bible? (*Notes for Parents for Day 27 may help.*)

**PRAY**
Thank God for the promise you chose. Ask Him to help you to trust Him to keep <u>all</u> His promises.

### Building up
Look up **Genesis 15v18** and **2 Samuel 7v10-11** to see God's promises for yourself.

## DAY 22
# Wise, wiser, wisest

Today's passages are:
**Table Talk:** 1 Kings 4v29-34
**XTB:** 1 Kings 4v29-34

**TABLE TALK**

Play **Hangman** to guess the word 'wisdom'.

**READ**

Today's verses are about Solomon's wisdom. As you read the passage, write down a 'W' each time you hear the words **wisdom**, **wise**, **wiser** or **wisest**.
**Read 1 Kings 4v29-34**

**TALK**

How many Ws did you write down? (*Probably 7 or 8 depending on which Bible version you are using.*) Why was Solomon's wisdom so amazing? (v29) (*Because God gave it to him.*)

Solomon knew all about plants, animals, birds, reptiles and fish! It sounds like Solomon loved using his wisdom to find out about God's fantastic world, and then tell others about it too.

**DO**

Choose something that God has made, and examine it closely (like Solomon did). It might be a flower from the garden, your pet hamster, or even your own hand!

**PRAY**

Now praise God for His wonderful handiwork.

***Table Talk Challenge:*** Spot as many things as possible today that God has made. Thank Him for each one of them.

### Building up
**Read Psalm 104**, which praises God for all of His creation. Notice God's wisdom in v24.

---

## DAY 23
# Only the best

Today's passages are:
**Table Talk:** 1 Kings 5v8-9, 6v37-38
**XTB:** 1 Kings 5&6

**DO**

Look at the picture. Take it in turns to guess what the man is doing and why.

**READ**

In his fourth year as king, Solomon started to build a temple for God. The walls and floors and ceilings were made of beautiful **cedar wood**. The wood came from Hiram, the king of Tyre. **Read 1 Kings 5v8-9** to see what the man on the raft was doing.

The outside of the temple was built of **stone**. The stone was shaped <u>before</u> it was brought to the temple so that there was no sound of hammering or cutting in the temple as it was being built. (*1 Kings 6v7*) The whole of the inside of the temple was covered in pure **gold**. Even the floors were gold! (*1 Kings 6v21&30*)
**Read 1 Kings 6v37-38**

**TALK**

How long did it take to build the temple? (v38) (*7 years*) Turn to **Notes for Parents** on the next page to see what the temple looked like.

Solomon had his best craftsmen working on the temple, using the best materials. Only the **best** would do. How can <u>you</u> give your best to God? (*It might involve your time, or money, or skills, or...*) Pray together about your answers.

**PRAY**

### Building up
Solomon's dad, David, had wanted to build a temple for God. But God told David it wasn't <u>his</u> job to build a temple—it would be his son's job to do it.
**Read 2 Samuel 7v1-5, 12-13**

# DAYS 23-24
## Notes for Parents

### DAY 23 – THE TEMPLE
The temple looked like this. It was about 30 metres long, 10 metres broad and 15 metres high. It was a magnificent building, beautifully decorated, and full of gold.

### DAY 24 – THE TEMPLE PILLARS
There were two massive bronze pillars outside Solomon's temple. They were called Jakin and Boaz. **Jakin** means 'God establishes'. **Boaz** means 'In God is strength'.

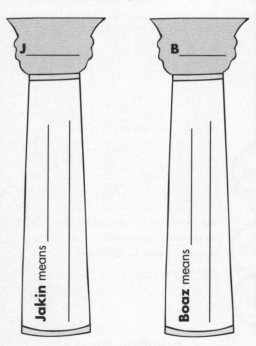

*Write the **names** on the top of the pillars, and what each name **means**.*

# DAY 24 · The promise & the power

Today's passages are:
**Table Talk:** 1 Kings 7v21-22
**XTB:** 1 Kings 7v21-22

**TABLE TALK**
What things do you have that remind you of God and Jesus? (*eg: posters with Bible verses, wearing a small cross, a 'What Would Jesus Do?' bracelet...*)

**READ**
Solomon had two HUGE reminders about God. Look again at the temple picture. Do you see the two bronze pillars outside the temple? They looked very impressive, but that's <u>not</u> the only reason they were there... **Read 1 Kings 7v21-22**

**DO**
What were the pillars called? (v21) (*Jakin/Jachin and Boaz.*) These names mean something important. Read about them in **Notes for Parents**, and then write the <u>names</u> on the pillars, and what each name <u>means</u>.

**THINK**
**Jakin:** God had promised David (Solomon's dad) that He would '<u>establish</u>' his kingdom for ever. That means that someone from David's family would be king for ever (2 Samuel 7v12-13).

**Boaz:** God had the <u>strength</u> to keep His promise about David's family line. And if Solomon (and other kings after him) were to be good kings, they needed to rely on God's <u>strength</u> to help them.

**PRAY**
Every time Solomon saw these pillars he would be reminded of **God's promise** and **God's power**. What can <u>you</u> use to remind you of God's promises and His power? (*Maybe stick something on either side of your door.*) Ask God to help you to trust His promises and rely on His strength.

## Building up
Read the full details of the pillars in **1 Kings 7v13-22**.

# DAY 25
# God is with us

Today's passages are:
**Table Talk:** 1 Kings 8v6-9
**XTB:** 1 Kings 8v1-9

**TABLE TALK**

**Recap:** How long did the temple take to build? (*7 years*) What was it made of? (*Stone and cedar wood, all lined with gold.*) What was outside the temple? (*Two bronze pillars, which reminded the people of God's promises and power.*)

**READ**

Now that the temple was finished, it was time to bring something very important into it... **Read 1 Kings 8v6-9**

**TALK**

What did the priests carry into the temple? (v6) (*The ark of the covenant/the covenant box.*) Where did they put it? (v6) (*The Most Holy Place*)

The ark of the covenant was a wooden box, covered in gold. Inside the ark were two stone tablets with the Ten Commandments written on them. The ark reminded the Israelites that **God was with them**.

Now that the ark was in the temple, it meant that the <u>temple</u> also reminded the people that God was with them.

**THINK**

Since Jesus, God's people don't need a temple. If you're a Christian (a follower of Jesus) then God is with <u>you</u> wherever you are. Think of some places where God is with you (*eg: at home, school, up a tree...*) Now thank God that He is with you in all these places—and everywhere else too!

**PRAY**

## Building up
The ark was made at the time of Moses. Read about it in **Exodus 25v10-22**.

---

# DAY 26
# Crowded by a cloud!

Today's passages are:
**Table Talk:** 1 Kings 8v10-13
**XTB:** 1 Kings 8v10-13

**DO**

Do you ever look at the clouds and try to make pictures from their shapes? Try it now—with <u>real</u> clouds if you can see any, or if not, draw some cloud shapes.

**READ**

Imagine turning up for a church service, and finding you can't go in because the building is full of cloud! That's what happened at the temple...
**Read 1 Kings 8v10-13**

**TALK**

What was the cloud a sign of? (v11) (*The cloud was a sign of God's presence. He had completely filled the temple with His glory!*)

Think of some words to describe a **thick** cloud.
When a cloud is thick, you can <u>see</u> it, but you can't see <u>through</u> it. The Israelites could see the cloud, so they knew that God was there, that He was <u>with</u> them. But they couldn't see God Himself.

**THINK**

God is too dazzling and wonderful for a human being to be able to look at Him. What's the best way for us to see God? Do you know what Jesus said about this? (*Jesus told His followers that they could see God by looking at Him [John 14v9]. As we read about Jesus in the Bible, He shows us what God is like.*)

**PRAY**

Ask God to help you to see Him and know Him more and more as you read the Bible together.

## Building Up
Once, when Moses asked to see God's face, all he saw was a glimpse of God's back. Anything more would have been too much for him! **Read Exodus 33v18-23**.

# Solomon speaks

# Notes for Parents

**KEYPOINT**
God kept all of the promises He made to David and Solomon. God <u>always</u> keeps His promises.

Today's passages are:
**Table Talk:** 1 Kings 8v14-21
**XTB:** 1 Kings 8v14-21

**TABLE TALK**

Can you think of any **promises** that have been made to you? Were they kept? How do you feel about broken promises?

**READ**

The temple was finished. The ark was in its place. The cloud had filled the temple. Now Solomon had some things to say. Listen out for what he said about <u>promises</u>... **Read 1 Kings 8v14-21**

**TALK**

Who had God made promises to? (v15) (*David, Solomon's dad.*) What had God promised? (v20) (*That David's son would be king after him, and would build the temple.*) Did God keep these promises? (*Yes*)

God kept <u>all</u> of the promises He had made to David and Solomon. God <u>always</u> keeps His promises.

Read about God's promises to us in **Notes for Parents** opposite.

**PRAY**

Use the words of these promises to help you to pray to God.

### Building up
Read the full extent of God's generous promises to David in **2 Samuel 7v4-16**. God promised that someone from David's family would be king for ever (v16). <u>Who</u> is the answer to this promise? (*Jesus, who comes from David's family line.*)

## THE PROMISE KEEPER

**'The Lord is faithful to all His promises.' Psalm 145v13**

'For God loved the world so much that He gave His only Son, so that everyone who believes in Him may not die but have eternal life.'
*John 3v16*

'Everyone who calls on the name of the Lord will be saved.' *Romans 10v13*

God has said, 'Never will I leave you; never will I forsake you.' *Hebrews 13v5*

'This Jesus, who was taken from you into heaven, will come back in the same way that you saw Him go to heaven.' *Acts 1v11*

'God will not let you be tempted beyond what you can bear. But when you are tempted, He will also provide a way out so that you can stand up under it.' *1 Corinthians 10v13*

'And we know that in all things God works for the good of those who love Him, who have been called according to His purpose.' *Romans 8v28*

And remember that God promises judgement too...
'I will punish the world for its evil, the wicked for their sins.' *Isaiah 13v11*

## DAY 28
# No one like God

## DAY 28-38
# Notes for Parents

**KEYPOINT**
There's no other god like the One true God. He always does what He says, and never lets us down.

Today's passages are:
**Table Talk:** 1 Kings 8v22-26
**XTB:** 1 Kings 8v22-26

**TABLE TALK**

Think of some words to describe God. (Choose at least two each.) Write them down for later.

**READ**

Today we're going to start reading Solomon's prayer when the temple was dedicated to God. He begins by praising God... **Read 1 Kings 8v22-26**

**TALK**

How does Solomon describe God? (v23) (*1—There's no god like God in heaven above or earth below. 2—God keeps His covenant with His people.*)

Check out '*covenant*' in the Bible dictionary in **Notes for Parents**.

**THINK**

Many people who lived near the Israelites prayed to pretend gods. They **hoped** these gods would hear them and be good to them—but they could never be **sure**. They were often disappointed. But it was different for the Israelites. How? (*They knew that their God was not only real, but always did what He said He would do.*)

The Israelites could **trust** God—and you can trust God too! He will always do what He says, and never let you down.

**PRAY**

There is no one like God. Praise Him using the words you wrote down.

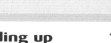

### Building up

You may want to use this opportunity to talk with your child about people who still follow pretend gods today. The Bible tells us about the One true God, and how we can know Him. The only way to be right with God is by trusting in **Jesus**. Pray for anyone you know from other religions. Ask God to give you an opportunity to tell them about Jesus.

### TABLE TALK BIBLE DICTIONARY

**C**

A **Covenant** is an agreement (a promise) that  mustn't be broken. God had made a covenant with the Israelites. He said He'd look after them and they said they'd obey Him.

**F**

**Festival of Shelters** (also called the Feast of Tabernacles) is a huge Jewish feast celebrating the end of the harvest, and God's goodness to His people.

**G**

**Grace** is God's HUGE kindness to people who don't deserve it. It is an <u>undeserved gift</u>. God's grace is seen all through the Bible, and most of all when He sends His own loved Son, Jesus, to take the punishment for our sins.

**P**

**Prayer** means talking to **G_____**. We can talk to God **any_____, any_____** about **any_____**.  God <u>always</u> hears us when we pray.

**S**

**Sacrifices** were gifts (usually animals or birds) given to God to say thank you or sorry to Him.

# DAY 29
# Phone a friend

**KEYPOINT**
We can talk to God anywhere, anytime about anything—and He hears us.

Today's passages are:
**Table Talk:** 1 Kings 8v27-30
**XTB:** 1 Kings 8v25-30

 **TABLE TALK**

Each think of a famous person you'd love to talk to. (*eg: a footballer, pop star, someone from the royal family...*)

Now imagine that they phone you up! How would you feel?

 **READ**

Today's Bible verses are about talking to someone fabulous and famous—but it's not a pop or sports star! Read about it in the next part of Solomon's prayer.
**Read 1 Kings 8v27-30**

 **TALK**

Yesterday we saw that there is <u>no one</u> like God. What else does Solomon say about God? (v27) (*The temple isn't fantastic enough to be God's house—nothing is good enough or great enough for God.*) Wow! God is awesome! But what does our amazing God do when we pray? (v30) (*He hears us!*)

 **THINK**

Have you ever stopped to think how fantastic that is??? God is the all-powerful Creator of our universe—but we can talk to Him **anywhere**, **anytime** about **anything**. And He <u>hears</u> us. That's loads better than a phone chat with David Beckham!

 **DO**

Look up '**prayer**' in yesterday's Bible dictionary, and fill in the gaps.

 **PRAY**

Thank God that you can talk to Him anywhere, anytime about anything. Tell Him how that makes you feel.

### Building up
Read some of Jesus' teaching about prayer in **Matthew 6v5-13**. God already knows what we need, so we don't need to babble! (v7)

---

# DAY 30
# Hear our prayers

**KEYPOINT**
If we tell God we are sorry for our sin, and ask Him to help us, He will always hear us.

Today's passages are:
**Table Talk:** 1 Kings 8v35-36
**XTB:** 1 Kings 8v31-53

 **TABLE TALK**

Take it in turns to <u>mime</u> situations when you would want to pray (*eg: when you're ill, worried, thankful, sorry...*)

 **READ**

In the second half of Solomon's prayer, he lists lots of stuff that might happen to the Israelites—and asks God to hear their prayers at all of those times. (*The list is in Building Up below if you want to go through it.*) Most of Solomon's examples were caused by **sin**. They would happen when the Israelites turned their backs on God and did what <u>they</u> wanted instead.
**Read 1 Kings 8v35-36**

 **TALK**

What problem are these verses about? (v35) (*No rain*) Why would God stop the rain? (v35) (*Because the people had sinned.*) What did Solomon ask God to do? (*Hear the people when they prayed for forgiveness; forgive them; teach them the right way to live; send rain.*)

 **THINK**

Solomon asked God to hear His people's prayers, even when their problems had been caused by their own sin! When <u>we</u> sin, it makes God sad and angry. But it needn't stop us from praying! If we tell God we are sorry, and ask Him to help us, He will always hear us.

 **PRAY**

Is there anything you need to say sorry to God for? Do so now, then thank Him that you are always able to pray to Him, even when you've let Him down.

### Building up
<u>Solomon's list:</u> **1**—When they sinned against someone (v31-32); **2**—When they were defeated by an enemy (v33-34); **3**—When there was no rain (v35-36); **4**—When there was disease or disaster (v37-40); **5**—When they went into battle (v44-45); **6**—When they were captured by their enemies (v46-50).

## DAY 31 All peoples on earth

Today's passages are:
**Table Talk:** 1 Kings 8v41-43
**XTB:** 1 Kings 8v41-43

 **DO**

Find your country in an atlas, or your town on a road map.

 **READ**

We're still reading about Solomon's prayer at the dedication of the temple. Part of his prayer is about us!!!
**Read 1 Kings 8v41-43**

 **TALK**

Solomon had just built the <u>Jewish</u> temple. But he included <u>non-Jews</u> in his prayer too, and asked God to hear them when they prayed. Who did Solomon want to hear about God? (v43) (*All the people of the earth.*)

 **THINK**

Today, there are Christians living in every part of the world! They come from <u>different countries</u>, and speak <u>different languages</u>, but they all love and obey the <u>same God</u>.

 **PRAY**

Thank God that the great message about Him is taught in <u>your</u> country too. And thank Him that you can always pray to Him—even if you spend your holidays in Paris, Peru, or Papua New Guinea!

### Building up
Choose a country from your atlas that has been in the news recently (maybe they're at war, or have suffered from a natural disaster, or have important elections coming up or...). Pray for that situation. And pray for the Christians who live there, asking God to help them to serve Him and to tell others about Him.

## DAY 32 God is our King

Today's passages are:
**Table Talk:** 1 Kings 8v54-61
**XTB:** 1 Kings 8v54-61

 **TABLE TALK**

(*You need pen and paper.*) After Solomon finished his prayer, he stood up and blessed the Israelites. As you read his words, make <u>two lists</u>: **1**—What God has done and what He is like; **2**—What Solomon asks God to do.

 **READ**

### Read 1 Kings 8v54-61

What does Solomon say about God in v60? (*The LORD is God—and there is no other.*) This means that God is the **King** of everything. What did Solomon say the Israelites must do? (v61) (*Obey God's commands.*)

 **DO**

(*Optional*) Copy v60 onto some paper, and put it where you'll see it this week.

Is God the King of <u>your</u> life? If He is, <u>you</u> need to obey His commands too.

 **PRAY**

Use your two lists to help you to pray. ***Praise*** God for what He is like, and ***ask*** Him to be with you and help you to obey Him as your King.

### Building up
Read **v56** again. Moses lived 300 years before Solomon. In that time, how many promises had God broken? (*None!*) Read some of those promises in **Exodus 3v14-22**.

# What's the point of parenting?

What's the point of parenting? I'm not talking about that feeling we all sometimes have of complete exasperation: that you have wasted your breath, effort and time yet again. No, I'm talking about the *End Point*. The thing we are aiming at, for and with our children. It's such an obvious question that it is very rarely asked because most parents do it by sheer instinct alone.

Surely our overall aim is to bring our children to maturity: to raise happy, healthy, capable children, who turn into happy, healthy, capable adults. It is a painful job, because at many stages children are so adorable and fun to be with, there can be a sense of loss as they move on. But as much as we may hate some parts of the job, the sense in it is obvious. We urge them to maturity in so many ways: physically through sport and exercise; intellectually through reading and discussion; socially through play and interaction with others; and emotionally through laughter, tears and honesty.

## SPIRITUAL MATURITY

But there is also a spiritual maturity that we need to help our children towards, and sadly, this is much less intuitive for us than the other areas. But the good news is that this is God's aim too. When Paul wanted to sum up what his aim in life was, he said this to his children in the faith living in Colossae:

*We proclaim Him (Jesus), admonishing and teaching everyone with all wisdom, so that we may present everyone mature in Christ.* **Colossians 1v28**

Notice the central connection of this verse. What leads to maturity is hearing about, appreciating and believing in Jesus Christ. Earlier in the same chapter he spells out in more detail what Spiritual maturity means:

*For this reason, since the day we heard about you, we have not stopped praying for you and asking God to fill you with the* <u>knowledge</u> *of his will through all* <u>spiritual</u> <u>wisdom</u> *and* <u>understanding</u>. *And we pray this in order that you may live a life worthy of the Lord and may please him in every way:* **bearing fruit in every good work,** *growing in the* <u>knowledge</u> *of God,* **being strengthened with all power according to his glorious might** *so that you may have* **great endurance and patience,** *and* **joyfully giving thanks to the Father,** *who has qualified you to share in the inheritance of the saints in the kingdom of light.* **Colossians 1v9-12**

Most of us know instinctively what is good for children. We may need encouraging from time to time to think about eating five portions of fruit and veg a day for a healthy diet, or walking to school for health. But we probably need much more encouragement to keep going at moving our children towards spiritual maturity. Here are some of the things that this passage suggests you ought to be doing to be a good Christian parent:

★ **Prayer:** the prime qualification for being a Christian parent is the recognition that we can't do it! Only God can save our children. Only the Spirit of God can bring them alive. Only through Jesus' life, death and resurrection can they be brought to spiritual maturity. We need, above all, to be parents who pray for our children daily. If you are able, pray with your spouse. Or pray for a moment outside their bedroom door as you go to bed yourself. And don't pray that their problems and difficulties will be taken away—that kind of prayer actually just demonstrates our own spiritual immaturity. Rather, ask for the things Paul asks for: that they would be filled with the wonder of the Gospel, grow to spiritual maturity, and be fruitful in good works.

★ **Teaching**: Paul lays emphasis on **knowledge** (with wisdom and spiritual understanding). Knowledge in the Bible is never just knowing facts, or being a Bible boffin. True knowledge involves knowing the truth, but also believing it and living by it. It is truth in action. So we will teach and **apply** the Bible to their lives.

And because being a disciple needs to be modelled in our lives, we will also show them how we are growing towards maturity as parents. We may ask them what they learned at Sunday School on the way home from church, but we will also share with them what we learned from the sermon, and ask them to pray for us, and help us in applying it to family life.

As you are reading *Table Talk* at this very moment you've clearly made a brilliant start in this—but don't stop there. Try to use any opportunity you have during the day to re-inforce, illustrate or to talk naturally about the Lord who loves us and gave Himself for us.

★ **Bearing fruit in every good work:** showing a loving care towards others needs to be part of the fabric of your lives. This is not only in small acts of kindness to neighbours and friends, but also in the way you talk about others (no gossip or backbiting), the way you spend your money and give to others, and the way that you show a willingness to forgive and put right broken relationships.

I find that I regularly need to ask forgiveness from my children for things I have done wrong, either to them, or in front of them. We are often at our most unguarded in front of the family, and they tend to see the worst of us (especially in the car, rushing to church!). Showing them that we are working to control the sin in our lives, will help them deal with their own struggles in the long run. But all this 'good work' needs to be set in the right context. It is all because 'God loves them, so we must too.' We show mercy because we have been shown mercy. We forgive, because we have

been forgiven.

★ **Depending on God**: And all this must be done in the power and strength of God. Even children can so easily turn into prigs and self-righteous hypocrites. One of my daughters is especially prone to smugly boasting of her finer points to anyone who will listen. By expressing our dependence on God, and giving Him the glory in prayer daily, we will guard against this, the worst disease of the religious.

★ **Endurance and patience**: Paul sees that consistency and 'stickability' is one of the great signs that someone has reached Christian maturity. It is also the quality that most children need from their parents. It is one of the reasons why regular Bible-reading habits are so important. We brush our teeth everyday because we believe it is good for us. It is often hard to get children to stick at it (not to mention us as adults!) but it is worth insisting on, because we know that in due season it will bring a harvest. They will thank you for helping them form Godly habits that stretch into adulthood.

> **The prime qualification for being a Christian parent is the recognition that we can't do it!**

★ **Joyful thanksgiving**: This is not just getting into the habit of 'saying your p's and q's' that most parents have a constant battle with. Thankfulness and joy are the badges of genuine Christian spirituality. Knowing our dependence on the grace of God, and being genuinely grateful for every gift, every breath, every plateful of food, and every opportunity to serve or even to suffer for the Lord who loves us and gave His life for us.

And the ultimate joy for us—far more than any degrees, or trophies or human achievements, will be if they are able to stand mature in Christ at the last.

**Tim Thornborough**
*(still striving to be mature in Christ)*

**KEYPOINT**
Solomon and co. had a party because God was so good to them.

Today's passages are:
**Table Talk:** 1 Kings 8v65-66
**XTB:** 1 Kings 8v62-66

**TABLE TALK**

How many reasons can you think of for having a party? (eg: birthday, new home, Christmas, wedding anniversary, retirement...)

**READ**

Solomon and co. had a party because <u>God was so good to them</u>. Their celebrations lasted at least a week! Check out **'Festival of Shelters'** in the Bible Dictionary on Day 28, and then read **1 Kings 8v65-66**

**TALK**

How long did the people celebrate for? (See v65) The people went home happy after their celebrations. Why were they so happy? (v66) (Because of all the good things God had done for them and for David ie: keeping the promises He had made to David in 2 Samuel 7v8-16.)

**PRAY**

Think of some ways that God has been good to <u>you</u>. (Choose at least three.) Now thank God for His goodness. Maybe you could have a party to celebrate!

### Building up
Read about **'sacrifices'** in the Bible Dictionary on Day 28, then read **1 Kings 8v62-64**. This was such a huge celebration that the usual altar was too small to cope!

**KEYPOINT**
Solomon had to choose whether to serve God or turn away from Him. We have the same choice.

Today's passages are:
**Table Talk:** 1 Kings 9v1-9
**XTB:** 1 Kings 9v1-9

**TABLE TALK**

**Flashback:** At the start of the story of Solomon, God appeared to Solomon and offered to give him whatever he wanted. What did Solomon ask for? (Wisdom).

**READ**

After the temple was finished, God appeared to Solomon again. As you read God's words, listen for what will happen if Solomon <u>obeys</u> God, and what will happen if he <u>doesn't</u>...
**Read 1 Kings 9v1-9**

**TALK**

What will happen if Solomon obeys God? (v5) (God will allow Solomon's family to rule Israel for ever.) What will happen if Solomon disobeys God? (v7) (God will remove the Israelites from the land of Israel, and abandon His temple.)

God has made things very clear to Solomon. If he serves God like his father David did, then God will <u>bless</u> him and his people. But if he turns away from God, he will be <u>punished</u>.

**THINK**

Ask your child what they think Solomon will do—will he serve God, or turn away from Him? We'll find out what Solomon does in the next few days.

**PRAY**

What about <u>you</u>? Do you want to love and serve God with every part of your life? Or are you in danger of making other things more important than God? Talk about this together—and then talk to God about your answers.

### Building up
Joshua made a similar challenge to the Israelites after they had settled in Israel. Read **Joshua 24v14-15**. Some families have v15 on display in their home: 'As for me and my household, we will serve the LORD.' You might like to do the same.

# DAY 35
# Wisdom and wealth

**KEYPOINT**
The Queen of Sheba came to hear Solomon's wisdom—and praised God for it.

Today's passages are:
**Table Talk:** 1 Kings 10v1-9
**XTB:** 1 Kings 10v1-13

**TABLE TALK**
Think about the leaders at your church, Sunday School or Christian group. What are they specially good at? (*Guitar playing, telling Bible stories, caring...*)

**READ**
When Solomon first became king, God gave him the <u>wisdom</u> he asked for. God gave him great <u>wealth</u> too. In today's verses, someone came to see these for herself. **Read 1 Kings 10v1-9**

**TALK**
Who came to see Solomon? (v1) (*The Queen of Sheba*) Why did she come? (v1) (*To test Solomon with hard questions.*) How many of her difficult questions did Solomon answer? (v3) (*All of them.*) The Queen of Sheba was <u>amazed</u> at all she saw and heard. Who did she give the praise to? (v9) (*God*)

**THINK**
The Queen of Sheba was <u>right</u> to praise God. **He** was the One who gave such wisdom and wealth to Solomon.

**PRAY**
Think again about the leaders at your church or group. It is **God** who has given gifts to your leaders. Praise and thank Him for them now.

### Building up
Solomon's riches were astonishing. Read about them in **1 Kings 10v14-25**. Note again the emphasis of the writer of 1 Kings (v24)—it was **God** who gave all this to Solomon.

---

# DAY 36 Greater than Solomon

**KEYPOINT**
Jesus is far wiser than Solomon. We must listen to Him, and obey His words.

Today's passages are:
**Table Talk:** Matthew 12v42
**XTB:** Matthew 12v42

**TABLE TALK**
What's the furthest you have travelled to go and see someone? Why did you go?

**READ**
The Queen of Sheba travelled 1000 miles to listen to Solomon's wisdom. She was very impressed. But, wise and wealthy though Solomon was, he was just a man. We're going to jump into the New Testament today to meet someone far more impressive than Solomon...
**Read Matthew 12v42**

**TALK**
The Queen of Sheba is called the Queen of the South by Jesus. What did she travel a huge distance to do? (v42) (*To listen to Solomon's wisdom.*) What did Jesus say about that? (v42) (*Someone greater than Solomon is here.*)

**THINK**
Jesus was talking about **Himself**. He's far more impressive than Solomon! Ask your child to finish these sentences:

- Solomon was wise, but Jesus is _____ (*wiser*)
- Solomon was great, but Jesus is _____ (*greater*)
- Solomon was king of Israel, but Jesus is King of _____ (*the world!*)

**PRAY**
The Queen of Sheba travelled a long way to listen to Solomon. But it's far better (and more important) to listen to King Jesus. Ask Him to help you listen to what He says in the Bible, and obey His words.

### Building up
This part of Matthew's Gospel is about the religious leaders demanding a <u>sign</u> from Jesus. But they had refused to believe the signs they had, and would be condemned by the Queen of Sheba (and others) for rejecting Jesus. **Read Matthew 12v38-42**.

## DAY 37
## Led astray...

> **KEYPOINT**
> Solomon married many wives from other nations, and turned away from God.

Today's passages are:
**Table Talk:** 1 Kings 11v1-6
**XTB:** 1 Kings 11v1-6

**DO** On seven small pieces of paper, write these words: *Do, not, marry, people, from, other, nations.* On eight other pieces, in another colour of pen, write: *The, king, is, not, to, have, many, wives.* Jumble the papers up, then ask your child to unjumble them to find two rules God gave to His people.

**READ** God gave both these rules for the same reason—so that His people wouldn't turn away from Him and start to worship other gods. These were <u>good</u> rules—but read what Solomon did...
**Read 1 Kings 11v1-6**

**TALK** Did Solomon marry women from other nations? (v1-2) (*Yes*) How many wives did Solomon have? (v3) (*700 wives! And 300 concubines/girlfriends.*) When did Solomon's wives turn his heart away from God? (v4) (*As he grew old.*)

It didn't happen straight away. But <u>slowly</u> Solomon changed, so that God wasn't 'No.1' in his life any more.

**THINK** Is God **No.1** in <u>your</u> life? What things or people might slowly become more important to you than loving and serving God?

**PRAY** Ask God to help you not to slip away from Him as Solomon did.

### Building up
Check out God's good rules for His people in **Deuteronomy 7v3-4** and **17v17-20**.

---

## DAY 38
## Solomon loved...

> **KEYPOINT**
> God <u>punished</u> Solomon for turning to other gods, but delayed because of <u>grace</u>.

Today's passages are:
**Table Talk:** 1 Kings 11v7-13
**XTB:** 1 Kings 11v7-13

**TABLE TALK** Play **hangman** to guess the phrase 'Solomon loved'.
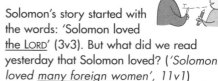

Solomon's story started with the words: 'Solomon loved <u>the LORD</u>' (3v3). But what did we read yesterday that Solomon loved? ('*Solomon loved <u>many foreign women</u>*', 11v1)

**READ** God's wasn't **No.1** in Solomon's heart any more. Instead, Solomon turned to other gods (the pretend gods his wives believed in). He even built places of worship for these pretend gods!
**Read 1 Kings 11v7-13**

**TALK** How did God feel about Solomon? (v9) (*Angry*) On Day 34 we read how God warned Solomon that he'd be punished if he turned away from God. What was God's punishment? (v11) (*He would take the kingdom away from Solomon and make someone else king instead.*) God was <u>right</u> to punish Solomon, but He also showed him **grace** (huge kindness). How? (v12-13) (*The punishment would be delayed until after Solomon's death, and his son would still rule over part of the kingdom.*)

*Check out **grace** in the dictionary on Day 28.*

**THINK** <u>All</u> sin must be punished. That includes <u>our</u> sin. But God showed His **grace** to us by sending His own Son Jesus to take the punishment we deserve. *(More on Day 40.)*

**PRAY** Say sorry to God for the times you have let Him down. Thank Him for sending Jesus to take your punishment, so that you can be forgiven.

### Building up
Remind yourselves of God's warning to Solomon in **1 Kings 9v6-9**.

# DAY 39
# God keeps His word

Today's passages are:
**Table Talk:** 1 Kings 11v14, 23, 26
**XTB:** 1 Kings 11v14-26

**TABLE TALK**

**Flashback One:** God had promised David that his son would become <u>king</u> after him. (2 Samuel 7v12-13) Did God keep that promise? (*Yes, King Solomon was David's son.*)

**Flashback Two:** God also told David that when his son did wrong, God would use other men to <u>punish</u> him. (2 Samuel 7v14) God kept His word about this too—He used <u>three men</u> to punish Solomon. Read the verses to discover their names:

**READ**

**Read 1 Kings 11v14** (Hadad the Edomite)

**Read 1 Kings 11v23** (Rezon son of Eliada)

**Read 1 Kings 11v26** (Jeroboam son of Nebat)

God used **Hadad**, **Rezon** and **Jeroboam** to punish Solomon—just as He said He would.

**THINK**

God <u>always</u> keeps His word. That means He always gives the good things He has promised. It also means that He always punishes when He says He will.

**PRAY**

God's words always come true. That means everything you read in the Bible is true. How does that make you feel? Talk to God about it.

## Building up
Re-read some of God's promises (including judgement) in **Notes for Parents** on Day 27.

---

# DAY 40
# King for ever

Today's passages are:
**Table Talk:** 1 Kings 11v41-43
**XTB:** 1 Kings 11v41-43

**READ**

### Read 1 Kings 11v41-43

For how long did Solomon rule as king? (v42) (*40 years*) Who became king after him? (v43) (*Rehoboam his son*) In the end, Rehoboam was only king of a <u>bit</u> of Israel—just as God had said.

**TALK**

Solomon had started out really well. What good things do you know about him? (*He <u>loved God</u> like his father David had done—Day 16; he asked God for <u>wisdom</u> to help him rule—Day 17; he built the <u>temple</u> for God—Day 23.*)

But how did Solomon let God down? (*He married many <u>foreign women</u>—Day 37; he <u>turned away</u> from God and built places of worship for pretend gods—Day 38.*)

**THINK**

God's people needed a king who would love <u>God</u> totally. They needed a king who would love <u>them</u> too, and show them how to live for God. 1000 years after Solomon, this kind of king was born. Who was He? (*King Jesus*)

**1** King Jesus lived a <u>perfect</u> life. He never let God down. **2** King Jesus <u>loves</u> His people—so much that He died for them! **3** King Jesus came back to life, and <u>rules today</u> as King of the world. **4** One day, King Jesus will <u>come back</u> to our world. And He will welcome His forgiven friends into His wonderful kingdom for ever.

**PRAY**

Thank King Jesus for these four things.

## Building up
Are you one of Jesus' forgiven friends, looking forward to Him coming back again? If you're not sure, read **Notes for Parents** on Day 13.

**KEYPOINT**
Jesus' miraculous feeding of the 5000 was a sign that He is the Son of God.

Today's passages are:
**Table Talk:** John 6v5-11
**XTB:** John 6v1-11

## JESUS' MIRACLES [DAY 41]

At the end of his book, John tells us <u>why</u> he wrote about Jesus' miracles:

> These are written so that you may believe that Jesus is the Christ, the Son of God, and that by believing you may have life in His name.
>
> John 20v31

John is saying that miracles are like *signposts*. They point to <u>who</u> Jesus is, so that we can believe in Him.

 **TABLE TALK**

Welcome back to John's Gospel. Chapter six includes two of Jesus' most famous miracles. Ask your child what Jesus' miracles are for, then read **Notes for Parents** about *Jesus' miracles*.

 **READ**

A huge crowd of people had followed Jesus. They wanted to see Him do more miracles. **Read John 6v5-9**

 **TALK**

What did Jesus ask Philip? (v5) (*'Where shall we buy bread for these people*?') Why did Jesus ask this? (v6) (*To test Philip.*) How did Philip answer? (v7) (*That loads of money couldn't buy enough bread.*) Andrew joined in too. How much food did he tell Jesus the boy had? (v9) (*5 loaves, 2 fish*) Did Andrew think this was enough to feed everyone? (v9) (*No*)

## BUILDING UP [DAY 41]

How many people did Jesus feed? (John 6v10) (*About 5000 men.*)

**Did You Know?** In Bible times, they just counted men and boys who were 12 or older. They didn't count the women or children. If we guess that each man had one woman and one child with him, then Jesus fed a crowd of around 15,000 that day! (See Matthew 14v21.)

 **READ**

Philip and Andrew didn't understand yet what the miracles showed about Jesus—that He is <u>God's Son</u>, and so can easily feed thousands of people...
**Read John 6v10-11**

**TALK**

What did Jesus do? (v11) (*Took the food, gave thanks to God, and gave it to the people.*) How much did they have to eat? (v11) (*As much as they wanted.*)

That's amazing! Jesus fed thousands of people with just one boy's packed lunch! This was a **sign** that Jesus was **God's Son**. Only God's Son could do such amazing things.

 **PRAY**

Jesus is God's Son. Thank Him that nothing is too difficult for Him.

**Building up**
Read **Notes for Parents** opposite.

# DAY 42
# Who is Jesus?

**KEYPOINT**
Jesus was 'the Prophet' Moses had spoken of. He had come to be King of people's lives.

Today's passages are:
**Table Talk:** John 6v12-15
**XTB:** John 6v12-15

**TABLE TALK**

<u>Recap yesterday's story:</u> How big was the crowd? (*5000 men, not counting women and children.*) How big was the boy's lunch? (*5 small loaves and 2 fish.*) How much did the people have to eat? (*As much as they wanted.*)

**READ**

Jesus had just fed thousands of people with a tiny picnic! It was a *signpost* pointing to the fact that Jesus is *God's Son*. **Read John 6v12-15**

**TALK**

How many baskets did the disciples fill with scraps? (v13) (*Twelve*) Who did the people think Jesus was? (v14) (*The Prophet who was to come into the world.*)

**DO**

Check out *'prophet'* and *'the Prophet'* in the dictionary opposite.

The people thought that Jesus was God's messenger that Moses had talked about. They were **right!** But what did they want Jesus to become? (v15) (*Their king*) They thought Jesus had come to kick the Roman rulers out of their country and take over as king. But they were **wrong!**

**THINK**

Jesus <u>had</u> come to be King. But King of their lives, not king of their country! And He <u>had</u> come to rescue them. But to rescue them from sin, not from the Romans!

**PRAY**

Is Jesus the King in charge of your life? Ask God to help you live your lives for Jesus.

## Building up
*'Jesus came to rescue people from sin, not the Romans!'* Can <u>you</u> explain how Jesus rescues us? Stuck? Then check out 'Think' on Day 47.

# DAY 42–50
# Notes for Parents

## TABLE TALK BIBLE DICTIONARY

### D

**Disciple** — Anyone who follows Jesus is a disciple. Jesus also had twelve close followers, called *'the disciples'* or *'the Twelve'*.

### E

**Eternal life** isn't just life for ever. It's knowing Jesus as our Friend and King <u>now</u> so that one day we will live with Him for ever. It's for everyone who believes and trusts in Jesus —the only One who can give it!

### H

**Holy Spirit** — The Bible teaches that there is <u>one</u> God, made of <u>three</u> persons—the Father, the Son (Jesus), and the Holy Spirit. So the Spirit is God. His special work is to help us learn about Jesus, believe in Jesus, and speak about Jesus to others.

### P

**Prophet** means 'messenger'. Prophets were messengers from God. (*Look up 'The Prophet' as well.*)

**The Prophet** — God promised that He would send another prophet like Moses, who would come from the Jews. *This promise is in Deuteronomy 18v14-18.*

## DAY 43
# Walking on what? Er?

**KEYPOINT**
Jesus walked on water—another sign that He is the Christ, the Son of God.

Today's passages are:
**Table Talk:** John 6v16-21
**XTB:** John 6v16-24

**TABLE TALK**

Talk about the things that scare you. (eg: spiders, thunder, the dark...)

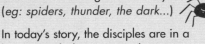

**READ**

In today's story, the disciples are in a boat on a dark, stormy night. But it's not the storm they're scared of—it's <u>Jesus</u>!
**Read John 6v16-21**

**TALK**

How did the disciples react when they saw Jesus walking on the water? (v19) (They were terrified.) But what did Jesus say to them? (v20) (Don't be afraid.)

The disciples saw something really scary —someone with superhuman power. What would He do to them?? But when they realised it was their great Friend Jesus they felt O.K.

**THINK**

This was another sign that Jesus is God's King (the Christ). He's totally powerful. If you don't know Him, you should be scared. But if Jesus is your King, He loves you. You don't need to be afraid of Him or anything else!

**PRAY**

Thank God that Jesus is the King. Ask Him to be yours too—so you don't need to be afraid of anything!

### Building up
**Read John 6v22-24**. The crowd couldn't work out how Jesus had crossed the lake without a boat! But we know how!

## DAY 44
# One way only

**KEYPOINT**
We must believe in Jesus. Good deeds aren't enough—only Jesus can give us eternal life.

Today's passages are:
**Table Talk:** John 6v25-29
**XTB:** John 6v25-29

**TABLE TALK**

<u>Recap:</u> What two miracles had Jesus just done? (Feeding 5000, Walking on water.) What were they signs of? (That Jesus was the Christ, the Son of God.)

**READ**

Crowds of people followed Jesus. They'd heard all about how He fed thousands of people with only five loaves and two fish. They were hoping He'd give <u>them</u> food too... **Read John 6v25-29**

**TALK**

What did Jesus say they should want more than bread? (v27) (Eternal life) Check out '**eternal life**' in the **Bible Dictionary** on Day 42.

Who could give them eternal life? (v27) (The Son of Man.) That means **Jesus**—and Jesus said that God was really pleased with Him (v27). How do we get eternal life? (v29) (Believe in the one God has sent.)

**THINK**

Lots of people think that doing good deeds is enough to get them to heaven. But Jesus says there's nothing <u>we</u> can **do** to get us into heaven. Good deeds aren't enough. We must **believe in Jesus**. Only <u>He</u> can give us eternal life.

**PRAY**

Don't trust in **good deeds**! Instead ask God to help you believe and trust in **Jesus** for eternal life. (This doesn't mean good deeds are wrong! But we do them to please God, not to get to heaven!)

### Building up
We read some other verses about eternal life in John 3. Check them out in **John 3v16** and **John 3v36**.

# DAY 45
# Bread from heaven

Today's passages are:
**Table Talk:** John 6v30-35
**XTB:** John 6v30-35

 **TABLE TALK**

Recap: What could Jesus give the crowd? (*Eternal life*) But what were they interested in? (*More food!*) **Read John 6v30-33**

 **TALK**

What did the crowd want to see? (v30) (*A miracle as a sign.*) They wanted a sign from Jesus, like the manna they ate at the time of Moses. But Jesus told them about something far more important than manna—the 'true bread from heaven', which is actually a person. Who gives this 'true bread'? (v32) (*God*) Where is this person from? (v33) (*Heaven*) What does he do? (v33) (*Give life to the world.*) Who does Jesus mean? (*Himself*)

 **READ**

There are seven famous sayings in John's Gospel, often called the 'I am' sayings. Jesus says one of them here: **read John 6v34-35**

 **THINK**

Jesus isn't talking about physical food to eat or water to drink. He means that if we trust in Him, He will give us <u>everything</u> we really need. He will forgive our sins! And give us everlasting life in heaven!

Have you trusted Jesus for those things? Do you really believe that He can give them to you?

**PRAY**

Thank God for giving us the best gift ever—Jesus!

## Building up
Check out the seven 'I am' sayings in John's Gospel:
**John 6v35**—'The bread of life'; **8v12**—'The light of the world'; **10v7**—'The gate'; **10v11**—'The good shepherd'; **11v25**—'The resurrection and the life'; **14v6**—'The way, the truth and the life'; **15v5**—'The vine'.

---

# DAY 46
# Never let go!

Today's passages are:
**Table Talk:** John 6v36-40
**XTB:** John 6v36-40

 **TABLE TALK**

(*You need to be sensitive in this discussion, but it could be very fruitful.*) Talk about any experience you have of broken friendships. (*Your child may well have the experience of falling out with friends; you may also know the pain of broken relationships yourself.*)

 **READ**

Jesus offers us a perfect friendship with Him—and it's one He will never break! **Read John 6v36-40**

 **TALK**

Jesus makes two promises about those who come to Him. What are they? (v37 & v39) (*v37—He will never turn them away; v39—He will never lose them.*)

That's fantastic! If we **come to Jesus** (that means trust and obey Him), then Jesus will never turn us away or lose us!

 **THINK**

That's so different to the broken relationships you were talking about before. How does it make you feel about your friendship with Jesus?

 **READ**

**Read v40 again**. What does Jesus promise to everyone who trusts in Him? (*Eternal life*) When Jesus returns to earth, everyone who has trusted Him will be raised back to life, to live with Him for ever!

 **PRAY**

There's lots to say thank you for in today's verses. Do that together now.

## Building up
Your child may have seen an older sibling or people in church give up on Christianity. Our confidence shouldn't be in the fact that we've 'become Christians', but in the fact that Jesus will never turn us away <u>if we come to Him</u>. But we have to come to Him and sometimes come back.

# DAY 47
## Death for life

**KEYPOINT**
Jesus gave up his life, so that we can have eternal life.

Today's passages are:
**Table Talk:** John 6v41-42, 48-51
**XTB:** John 6v41-51

**TABLE TALK**
Have you ever been told something that was hard to believe? Talk about it.

**READ**
Jesus looked like an ordinary man, so the people found it hard to believe what He said about coming from heaven.
**Read John 6v41-42**

Who did the people know? (v42) (*Joseph and Mary, Jesus' parents.*) They knew Jesus' family, so they didn't believe that He could give them eternal life.

**READ**
But Jesus told them again that He is 'the bread of life', and told them something amazing about that 'bread'...
**Read John 6v48-51**

**TALK**
The Israelites had eaten manna from God—but what still happened to them? (v49) (*They died.*) But Jesus is offering eternal <u>life</u>! He then explains that the 'bread of life' is His flesh (body). What will He do with it? (v51) (*Give it for the life of the world ie: He would die.*)

**THINK**
Jesus had to **die** so that we can have eternal life. We deserve to die for all the wrong things we've done. But Jesus took the punishment in our place. He **died** so that we can **live** for ever!

**PRAY**
Is there anything you want to thank Jesus for? Anything you want to tell Him?

### Building up
For the free booklet **Why did Jesus die?** write to Table Talk, The Good Book Company, 37 Elm Road, New Malden, Surrey, KT3 3HB. Or email: alison@thegoodbook.co.uk

# DAY 48
## Food for thought

**KEYPOINT**
We must eat to live, and we must trust Jesus for eternal life.

Today's passages are:
**Table Talk:** John 6v52-59
**XTB:** John 6v52-59

**TABLE TALK**

Put some bread on the table. Why do we eat food? (*eg: because it tastes great, to give us energy, to keep mum happy!*)

**READ**
The most important reason for eating is to **live**. Jesus said He was the **bread of life**. The crowd got confused and thought He meant they should actually eat Him!! **Read John 6v52-59** and listen out for something that Jesus keeps repeating.

**TALK**
What did Jesus keep saying? (*That we must feed on Him/eat His flesh and drink His blood.*) This must be really important if Jesus keeps repeating it! But He doesn't mean that people have to eat Him! There's a clue in v58—what will 'feeding on Jesus' give us? (v58) (*Eternal life.*)

Jesus gave up His own life so that we can have **eternal life**. Trusting in Jesus is a bit like eating. We must eat to live, and we must trust Jesus for eternal life.

**THINK**
It's crazy to give up food. Why? (*We would die! No food = death.*) Similarly, it's crazy to give up trusting Jesus. Why? (*No Jesus = no eternal life.*) Nothing's more important!

**PRAY**
Ask God to help you to fully trust in Jesus. To truly believe that Jesus' death makes is possible for you to have eternal life.

### Building up
We remember Jesus' death for us when we eat bread and drink wine during communion/the Lord's supper.
Read Jesus' words about that in **Matthew 26v26-28**.

# DAY 49 Time to turn back?

Today's passages are:
**Table Talk:** John 6v60-66
**XTB:** John 6v60-66

 **TABLE TALK**

Check out **'disciple'** in the Bible Dictionary on Day 42.

 **READ**

Jesus said He was the **bread of life**—the <u>only</u> way to eternal life. Many of Jesus' followers wouldn't believe Him. (In today's Bible verses, **disciples** means <u>all</u> of Jesus' followers, not just the twelve disciples.) **Read John 6v60-63**

 **TALK**

'The Son of Man' is a title for Jesus. What do you think v62 means? (*Jesus going back to heaven—which He did after being killed on the cross and coming back to life again.*) Who did Jesus say gives life? (v63) (*The Spirit*) What counts for nothing? (v63) (*Flesh/human power.*)

 **THINK**

These people were only interested in **earthly things**—food, money, living a good life. They weren't really interested in **spiritual things**—forgiveness, knowing God, eternal life. That's why they wouldn't believe Jesus. But only <u>Jesus</u> could give them eternal life!

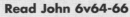

**Read John 6v64-66**

What did many of Jesus' followers do? (v66) (*Turned back.*) They refused to believe Jesus and live His way.

 **PRAY**

Do you know anyone who won't have anything to do with Jesus? Ask God to turn their lives around, so that they come to love Jesus and live His way. Pray this for yourselves too, if you're only into earthly things!

## Building up
Can you think of other Bible characters who turned back from following God? (eg: Solomon—Day 37; Judas—John 18v1-5.)

# DAY 50 The choice is yours

Today's passages are:
**Table Talk:** John 6v67-71
**XTB:** John 6v67-71

 **TABLE TALK**

In his book about Jesus, John has given us loads of **signposts** to help us believe that Jesus is the Christ (God's chosen King), the Son of God. Can you think of some of those signposts?

Now that we've read about the signposts, we have a choice:

• Believe Jesus, live for Him and have eternal life. *OR...*

• Don't believe Jesus, turn away from Him and live your own way.

Jesus' twelve disciples had that same choice...

 **READ**

**Read John 6v67-71**

 **TALK**

What did Simon Peter say to Jesus? (v68-69) (*You have the words of eternal life/We believe that you are the Holy One of God.*) Peter knew that trusting Jesus was the only way to have eternal life. And he believed that Jesus had been sent by God.

 **THINK**

How about you? Do you believe those things? Do you trust Jesus to give you eternal life? Or will you turn away like Judas did?

Tell God how you honestly feel. And ask Him to help you to really trust Jesus and live His way.

## Building up
In this issue of Table Talk we've read chapters 4, 5 and 6 of John's Gospel. Flick back through those chapters again to remind yourselves of what you've read. Thank God for the things you've learnt from John's book.

# DAY 51
# Rain, rain, go away

Today's passages are:
**Table Talk:** 1 Kings 17v1-6
**XTB:** 1 Kings 17v1-6

## King Solomon

Solomon had started out really well. He asked God for wisdom and built the temple for God.

But Solomon married many foreign women, against God's laws. Then he turned away from God to serve the pretend gods his wives believed in.

As a result, God said that the kingdom would be taken away from Solomon's family—but that Solomon's son would still be king of <u>part</u> of it (1 Kings 11v9-13).

## THE TWO KINGDOMS

God's words to Solomon came true:

• The Israelites were split into **two** kingdoms.

• The northern kingdom was called **Israel**.

• The southern kingdom was called **Judah**.

We're going to read about the northern kingdom of Israel. They'd had a whole bunch of bad kings, but their new king was the worst of all...

## King Ahab

King Ahab was the most evil king of Israel. He sinned far more than any king before him. He even built a temple for the pretend god Baal, and then served Baal instead of God! (1 Kings 16v29-33)

 **TABLE TALK**

Welcome back to the book of 1 Kings. Which king did we read about last time? (*Solomon*) Read **Notes for Parents** to find out what happened next.

 **READ**

Ahab was the most evil king of Israel. But God cared for His people, the Israelites. So God sent them one of His **prophets** (God's messengers). His name was <u>Elijah</u>.
**Read 1 Kings 17v1**

What did Elijah tell Ahab? (v1) (*There would be no dew or rain for the next few years.*)

 **THINK**

Who did King Ahab worship? (*Baal*) Baal was supposed to be the god of rain and storms. By stopping the rain, God showed that **He** is the <u>real</u> God of Israel, and that Baal was fake and powerless!

 **READ**

Elijah was in danger from King Ahab, so God told him to hide out for a while.
**Read 1 Kings 17v2-6**

 **TALK**

God made sure that Elijah had the food and water he needed. Where did they come from? (*The water from a brook. The food was brought by ravens!*)

 **PRAY**

God was going to use Elijah to teach King Ahab and the Israelites some very important things. Ask God to help <u>you</u> to learn more about Him too as you read about Elijah in 1 Kings.

**Building up**
Read about King Ahab in **1 Kings 16v29-33**.

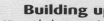

# DAY 52
## Notes for Parents

### THE WIDOW AT ZAREPHATH
Taken from 1 Kings 17v7-13

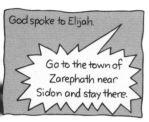

God spoke to Elijah.

Go to the town of Zarephath near Sidon and stay there.

I have commanded a widow who lives there to feed you.

So Elijah went to Zarephath, and found the widow gathering sticks.

Please bring me a drink of water.

And please bring me some bread.

As surely as the Lord your God lives, I tell you the truth.

I have no bread.

I have only a handful of flour in a jar and a little olive oil in a jug.

I have come here to gather some wood. I will take it home and cook our last meal.

My son and I will eat it – and then die from hunger.

But Elijah had good news for her...

Don't be afraid!

# DAY 52
## How to bake bread

**KEYPOINT**
God sent Elijah to a widow for food, then made sure that her oil and flour never ran out.

Today's passages are:
**Table Talk:** 1 Kings 17v13-16
**XTB:** 1 Kings 17v7-16

**TABLE TALK**

**Recap:** What had Elijah told Ahab? (*There'd be no rain for a few years.*) Then Elijah hid from Ahab. Where did his food and water come from? (*A brook and ravens.*)

God had stopped the rain, so Elijah drank water from a brook. But then the brook dried up! Read the picture story in **Notes for Parents**.

Elijah told the widow not to be afraid.

**READ**

**Read 1 Kings 17v13-16** to find out why.

**TALK**

What was God's message to the widow? (v14) (*The jar of flour will not be used up, and the jug of oil will not run dry until the day the LORD gives rain on the land.*) Did God's words come true? (v16) (*Yes*)

**THINK**

Do you think it was easy for that widow to trust God? Why/why not?

**PRAY**

Do <u>you</u> find it easy to trust God? Why/why not? Talk to Him about your answer.

### Building up
Read the whole story in **1 Kings 17v7-16**. This section of 1 Kings makes repeated references to 'the word of the LORD' eg: v8, v14, v16, v24. Why do you think that is?

# DAY 53
## True and powerful

**TABLE TALK**

Re-read yesterday's picture story. How did the story end? (*God gave the widow never-ending flour and oil to make bread with, just as He said He would.*)

**READ**

God was clearly looking after the widow and her son, as well as Elijah. But then her son became ill...
**Read 1 Kings 17v17-24**

**TALK**

What happened to the widow's son? (v17) (*He died.*) Elijah carried the dead boy up to his room, and cried out to God for help. What was his prayer? (v21) ('*O LORD my God, let this boy's life return to him.*') How did God answer Elijah's prayer? (v22) (*He brought the boy back to life.*)

**THINK**

How do you think his mum felt?

What did she say? (v24) ('*Now I know that you are a man of God and that the word of the LORD from your mouth is the truth.*')

**PRAY**

The widow was right! God's words are <u>always</u> true. Thank God that His words in the Bible are both true and powerful.

### Building up
All through the story of Elijah, there's a kind of competition between Baal and God. And <u>every</u> time: **GOD WINS!!!** This widow lived near Sidon, which was outside the kingdom of Israel. Ahab's wife Jezebel came from there: read **1 Kings 16v31**. This was <u>Baal</u> territory—but it was **God** who gave the widow never-ending food, and brought her son back to life—not Baal. ***God wins!***

# DAY 54
## Two ways to serve

**TABLE TALK**

Think of some people at church with up-front jobs (*eg: preaching*). Now think of people who do quiet background jobs (*eg: making tea, putting out chairs.*)

**READ**

King Ahab and the Israelites had been worshipping <u>Baal</u> instead of <u>God</u>. So God punished them by sending no rain for three whole years! **Read 1 Kings 18v1**

What was God going to do? (v1) (*Send rain.*)

Evil King Ahab had been searching for Elijah for three years, but God had kept him safely hidden. Ahab's wife, Jezebel, <u>hated</u> the followers of God. She had killed many of the prophets (God's messengers).

**READ**

Not all of Ahab's men were enemies of God. One of them had been helping God's prophets. **Read 1 Kings 18v2-8**

**TALK**

What had Obadiah done? (v4) (*Rescued 100 prophets.*) What did Ahab send Obadiah to look for? (v5) (*Grass for the animals.*) Who did he find instead? (v7) (*Elijah*) *Tomorrow we'll see what happens when Ahab and Elijah meet up...*

**Elijah** was God's messenger and boldly told people what God had to say. **Obadiah** served God secretly and bravely saved 100 prophets. Elijah and Obadiah served God in different ways.

**PRAY**

Ask God to show you how <u>you</u> can serve Him best.

### Building up
**Read 1 Kings 18v9-15** Obadiah was worried that Elijah would hide again, but he agreed to tell Ahab that Elijah was here.

# DAY 55
## Carmel contest

**KEYPOINT**
Elijah told the people they had to choose who to follow—Baal or God.

Today's passages are:
**Table Talk:** 1 Kings 18v16-21
**XTB:** 1 Kings 18v16-21

**TABLE TALK**

There's an important question running through chapter 18 of 1 Kings. Play **hangman** to find out what it is. (*The question is: 'Who is the real God?'*)

**READ**

The Bible shows us again and again that **God** is the One true God. But Ahab and the Israelites have been worshipping **Baal** instead! So now it's crunch time—a contest between Baal and God, at the top of Mount Carmel...
**Read 1 Kings 18v16-18**

What did Ahab call Elijah? (v17) (*Troubler of Israel.*) But who had really made trouble for Israel? (v18) (*Ahab—he'd led the people to worship Baal instead of God.*)

Elijah told Ahab to bring all of the Israelites to the top of Mount Carmel. He was to bring the 450 prophets of Baal too. **Read 1 Kings 18v19-21**

What choice did Elijah give the people? (v21) (*To follow Baal or follow God.*)

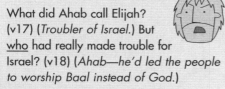
**THINK**

Like these people, we must choose what to do. Believing in God means **following** Him—doing what He wants. Do you follow God like that? If you follow what you or others want, you don't believe the LORD is God. Ask Him to help you do what He wants in every part of your life.

**PRAY**

### Building up
God had clearly told His people not to worship other gods: **read Exodus 20v1-6**. God said He would punish His people for serving other gods (v5). How had He punished Ahab and the Israelites? (*By stopping the rain for three years.*)

# DAY 56
## Baal fails

**KEYPOINT**
The prophets of Baal shouted, danced and cut themselves. But there was no answer. Baal fails!

Today's passages are:
**Table Talk:** 1 Kings 18v22-29
**XTB:** 1 Kings 18v22-29

**TABLE TALK**

It's time for the Carmel contest. Elijah has set a test for both Baal and God. Two stone altars are built, with wood for a fire and a sacrifice (gift) of meat on top. One altar is for Baal and one is for God. Whoever can set the sacrifice on **fire** is the true God. *Look at the pictures in* **Notes for Parents** *on the next page to see what the altars were like.*

**READ**

Elijah told the prophets of Baal that they could go first.
**Read 1 Kings 18v22-26**

**TALK**

What did Elijah say to the people? (v24) (*'The god who answers by fire—He is God.'*) Was there an answer from Baal? (v26) (*No!*) When there was no answer, Elijah made fun of the prophets of Baal. He told them to shout louder!
**Read 1 Kings 18v27-29**

Was there an answer from Baal this time? (v29) (*No!*)

**DO**

Write '**No answer**' across the picture of Baal's altar on the next page.

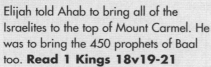

Elijah suggested that Baal wasn't answering because he was asleep! (v27) But the One true God isn't like that. Psalm 121 reminded the Israelites that God was their protector, who 'never dozes or sleeps' (Ps 121v4). That's true today too.

**THINK**

Thank God that He is always looking after you, and never asleep, no matter what time of day (or night!) it is.

**PRAY**

### Building up
Read **Psalm 121**, and notice how very different God is from Baal. Use the words of this psalm to thank and praise God.

## The two altars
### (Days 56 & 57)

**Baal's altar**

**God's altar**

## Elijah's last journey
### (Day 64)

Elijah was God's prophet (messenger). God used Elijah to show King Ahab and the Israelites that **God** is the One true God. At the end of Elijah's life, he walked around parts of Israel with **Elisha**, who would become prophet after him.

They walked from **Gilgal**, to **Bethel**, to **Jericho** and then to the **Jordan river**. *Check out the map to see their route.*

---

**KEYPOINT**
God sent fire to burn up His altar—and the Israelites saw that <u>He</u> is the real God.

Today's passages are:
**Table Talk:** 1 Kings 18v30-39
**XTB:** 1 Kings 18v30-39

**TABLE TALK**

**Recap:** What test had Elijah set up for Baal and God? (*Two altars were built. Whoever can set the sacrifice on fire is the true God.*) The prophets of Baal had spent all day shouting, dancing and cutting themselves. Was there an answer from Baal? (*No!*)

**READ**

Now it was Elijah's turn...
**Read 1 Kings 18v30-35**

**TALK**

Elijah rebuilt God's altar, using twelve stones for the twelve Israelite tribes. He was reminding the Israelites that **God was their God**, and they were <u>His</u> people. What did Elijah pour over the altar? (v33) (*Water*) How many times? (v34) (*Three times.*)

Why do you think Elijah poured water over everything?

**DO**

*Draw* water dripping from the wood and meat on God's altar, and filling a trench round the altar.

**READ**

The wet wood would be hard to set on fire. But <u>nothing</u> is too hard for God!!!
**Read 1 Kings 18v36-39**

**DO**

What did God do? (v38) (*Sent fire.*) *Draw* God's fire burning up the meat, the wood and even the stones!

What did the people cry out? (v39) ('*The LORD—He is God!*')

**PRAY**

Nobody and nothing can compete with God! Praise Him now.

### Building up
**Read 1 Kings 18v40**. The prophets of Baal had led the people away from God, so they were rightly punished—by death.

# DAY 58
## Fire proof

**KEYPOINT**
God sent rain—just as He had promised.

Today's passages are:
**Table Talk:** 1 Kings 18v41-46
**XTB:** 1 Kings 18v40-46

**TABLE TALK**

What's the weather like today? Is it likely to rain later? How can you tell?

**READ**

God had stopped the rain in Israel for three years. Why? (*To punish Ahab and the Israelites for worshipping Baal instead of God.*) But what did God say in **1 Kings 18v1**? (*He will send rain.*) Now that the Carmel contest was over, the time had come for God to send rain.
**Read 1 Kings 18v41-46**

**TALK**

How many times did Elijah send his servant to look towards the sea? (v43) (*Seven times*)  What did the servant see at last? (v44) (*A cloud as small as a man's hand.*) Elijah warned Ahab to set off for home before the rain stopped him. How much rain was there—a drizzle? or a downpour? (v45) (*A downpour.*) God had sent rain, <u>just as He promised</u>. What did Elijah do? (v46) (*Ran in front of Ahab's chariot all the way.*)

**THINK**

Think back over the story of the Carmel contest, and choose some words to describe God.

**PRAY**

Now use those words to praise and thank God.

---

### Building up
On Day 30, we read Solomon's prayer when he dedicated the temple. Re-read the part about 'no rain': **read 1 Kings 8v35-36**. How has God answered this prayer in chapter 18? (eg: v18, v39, v45.)

---

# DAY 59
## Broom gloom

**KEYPOINT**
Elijah felt awful—and wanted to die. But God took care of him.

Today's passages are:
**Table Talk:** 1 Kings 19v1-8
**XTB:** 1 Kings 19v1-8

**DO**

(*You need pen and paper.*) **Draw a happy face**. Think back over the Carmel contest. What was there to be happy about? (*The people had seen that God is the real God—not Baal. God had kept His promise to send rain.*)

**READ**

But not everyone was happy! **Draw an angry face**. Queen Jezebel (Ahab's wife) was a follower of Baal. When she heard what had happened on Mount Carmel—and that the 450 prophets of Baal had been killed—she was furious...
**Read 1 Kings 19v1-3**

**TALK**

Jezebel was out to **kill** Elijah! What did Elijah do? (v3) (*Ran for his life.*)

We don't know for sure why Elijah ran away. Maybe he had stopped trusting God. Maybe he was exhausted after the contest on Mount Carmel, and couldn't face another fight. But we do know how he felt later... **Read 1 Kings 19v4-8**

How did Elijah feel? **Draw his face**. It was too much for Elijah—he just wanted to die! But who did God send to help him? (v5) (*An angel.*) What did the angel give Elijah? (v6) (*Food and water.*) The food gave Elijah the strength he needed for his l-o-n-g journey. *Tomorrow we'll see what happened when he got there.*

**PRAY**

God took care of Elijah. No matter how <u>bad</u> things are, or how <u>sad</u> you feel, you can <u>always</u> turn to God. Talk to Him now.

---

### Building up
Do you know anyone who is feeling awful right now? Maybe because of illness, or the death of someone they loved, or depression. Pray for them now, and then find a way to let them know you're praying for them.

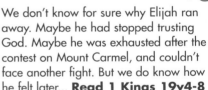

# DAY 60
## Listen carefully

**KEYPOINT**
God spoke to Elijah in a gentle whisper. He speaks to us through His Word, the Bible.

Today's passages are:
**Table Talk:** 1 Kings 19v9-14
**XTB:** 1 Kings 19v9-14

**TABLE TALK** Sit very quietly for a minute. What can you hear?

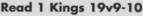

Elijah had run away from Jezebel, who wanted to kill him. God had kept Elijah alive, and now he was hiding in a cave. What do you think Elijah could hear?

**READ** Then Elijah heard God speaking to him. God had a question for Elijah...
**Read 1 Kings 19v9-10**

**TALK** What was God's question? (v9) (*'What are you doing here, Elijah?'*) Elijah told God how the Israelites were breaking His covenant laws. Elijah felt like he was the only godly person left. Check out **'covenant'** in the dictionary on Day 28.

**READ** Then God told Elijah to leave the cave...
**Read 1 Kings 19v11-14**

**TALK** What did Elijah hear and see? (v11-12) (*Wind, earthquake, fire, gentle whisper.*) Was God in the wind? (*No*) Was He in the earthquake? (*No*) Was He in the fire? (*No*) Was He in the gentle whisper? (*Yes*)

**THINK** Sometimes, God speaks to His people through spectacular things (like the fire on Mount Carmel). But He often speaks quietly, through His Word. For Elijah that meant a **voice**. What does it mean for us? (*The Bible.*)

**PRAY** Every day this week, pray before you start Table Talk, and ask God to speak to you from His Word. Thank Him now for what He's been saying in the past few days.

### Building up
**Read 2 Timothy 3v16-17** about God's Word to us—the Bible.

# DAY 61
## Judgement and grace

**KEYPOINT**
God used three men to punish the Israelites, but kept 7000 of them safe because of His grace.

Today's passages are:
**Table Talk:** 1 Kings 19v15-18
**XTB:** 1 Kings 19v15-18

**TABLE TALK** Look at today's heading. What do you think today's story is about? (*Judgement and grace.*) **Judgement** means God makes sure that sin is punished. **Grace** is God's HUGE kindness to people who don't deserve it. Listen out for both in today's story.

**READ** God is still speaking to Elijah on Mount Sinai (also called Horeb). God told Elijah to appoint three men who would punish Ahab and the Israelites for disobeying God. **Read 1 King 19v15-18**

**TALK** Who were the three men? (v15-16) (*Hazael, Jehu and Elisha.*) Ahab and the Israelites had disobeyed God. So God would use Hazael, Jehu and Elisha to punish them. This was God's **judgement**.

Did you spot God's **grace**? (*It's in v18.*) Even though the Israelites kept disobeying God, He would keep 7000 of them safe. That's fantastic grace!

**DO** Check out **'grace'** in the Bible dictionary on Day 28.

**PRAY** Think of some ways that God has shown His grace to you. (*eg: answering your prayers, sending Jesus...*) Thank God for these things now.

### Building up
An old way of explaining **grace** goes like this: **G**od's **R**iches **A**t **C**hrist's **E**xpense. What do you think this means? (*eg: Christ paid the price for our sins, by dying for us, so that we can be friends with God and live with Him in heaven.*)

# DAY 62
# God's character

**KEYPOINT**
Judgement and grace are two sides of God's character. They both have to be there.

Today's passages are:
**Table Talk:** John 5v24
**XTB:** John 5v24

**TABLE TALK**
Ask your child what there is on the two sides of a coin. Look at a few different coins to see the answer.

**DO**
Yesterday we saw two sides of God's character—**judgement** and **grace**. They seem quite different, but they <u>both</u> have to be there—like the two sides of the same coin. Cut out a coin shape from paper. Write 'Judgement—God makes sure that sin is punished' on one side, and 'Grace—God's HUGE kindness to people who don't deserve it' on the other.

The Bible tells us that God never changes (Malachi 3v6). That means He is the God of judgement and grace <u>today</u> as well.

**THINK**
We all **sin** (we all do what <u>we</u> want instead of what <u>God</u> wants). God's right **judgement** of our sin is that it must be punished. But God has also shown His **grace** to us. How? Talk about your answer, and then check it by reading Jesus' words in **John 5v24**.

How has God shown us His grace? (*By sending His own Son Jesus to save us.*)

**PRAY**
Have you been rescued by Jesus? If you have, you'll want to tell your friends about Jesus too. Ask God to help you to do that this week.

## Building up
**Read Malachi 3v6**. God <u>never</u> changes, so all the things you've read about Him in the book of 1 Kings are still true today. Write out the first part of this verse, and display it next to the coin you made today.

# DAY 63
# Farewell to farming

**KEYPOINT**
Elisha left farming to become Elijah's servant. Later, Elisha would be the next prophet.

Today's passages are:
**Table Talk:** 1 Kings 19v19-21
**XTB:** 1 Kings 19v19-21

**TABLE TALK**
<u>Recap:</u> What was Elijah's job? (*He was God's prophet, which means messenger.*) God had told Elijah to appoint **Elisha**. He was to be the next prophet after Elijah...

**READ**
**Read 1 Kings 19v19-21**

**TALK**
What was Elisha doing? (v19) (*Ploughing*) What did Elijah do? (v19) (*Threw his cloak around Elisha—a sign that Elisha would take his place as prophet.*) What did Elisha say? (*See v20*) What did Elisha do with his ploughing equipment? (v21) (*He burnt it, and turned his oxen into steaks for the people.*) This showed that Elisha was serious about his change of job.

Elisha was to be Elijah's servant. That meant doing stuff like pouring water on Elijah's hands before a meal (2 Kings 3v11). Not very exciting stuff! But **God** had called Elisha to do it, so he threw himself into it straight away.

**THINK**
Sometimes God wants us to serve Him in <u>little</u> things. (*Helping out at home, doing the cleaning at church, etc.*) But it's still serving God, and it still pleases Him!

**PRAY**
Think of some ways that you can serve God this week. Now ask Him to help you to get stuck into serving Him, even in the less exciting jobs.

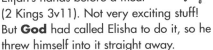

## Building up
Jesus was the King of Kings, but He also came to be a <u>servant</u>. **Read Mark 10v42-45**.

## DAY 64
# Time to go

**KEYPOINT**
God parted the water for Elijah and Elisha. Elisha wanted to serve as God's messenger.

Today's passages are:
**Table Talk** : 2 Kings 2v1-10
**XTB** : 2 Kings 2v1-10

**TABLE TALK**

We're going to jump into the book of **2 Kings** to finish the story of Elijah. As we join them, Elijah and Elisha are visiting lots of spots in Israel...
**Read 2 Kings 2v1-6**

**DO**

Which four places did they visit? (v1—Gilgal; v2—Bethel; v5—Jericho; v6—Jordan river.) Turn to **Notes for Parents** next to <u>Day 57</u> to find out more about **Elijah's last journey**.

Elijah and Elisha needed to cross the Jordan river... **Read 2 Kings 2v7-10**

**TALK**

What did Elijah do? (v8) (*Struck the water with his cloak.*) What happened? (v8) (*The water divided and they crossed on dry land.*)

Elisha wanted to carry on Elijah's work after he was gone. He wanted to serve God as His messenger to the Israelites. That's what v9 means. What did Elijah say about this? (v10) (*It would happen if Elisha saw Elijah going up to heaven.*) We'll read the answer to that <u>tomorrow</u>.

**PRAY**

We are <u>all</u> called to serve God. The Bible tells us loads of ways to do that. Ask God to help you serve Him, and to show you any special jobs He has just for you.

### Building up
Can you think of any other times when God dried up water so that His people could cross? (*Parting the Red Sea so Moses and the Israelites could escape from the Egyptians—Exodus 14v21-22; drying up the Jordan river so Joshua and the Israelites could cross into the promised land of Canaan—Joshua 3v14-17*).

---

## DAY 65
# Chariot of fire

**KEYPOINT**
Elijah went to heaven. God gave Elisha three signs that he was to be God's prophet after Elijah.

Today's passages are:
**Table Talk** : 2 Kings 2v11-15
**XTB** : 2 Kings 2v11-18

**TABLE TALK**

<u>Recap:</u> What did Elijah and Elisha do in yesterday's story? (*Walked round parts of Israel, then crossed the Jordan river on dry ground.*)

**READ**

Yesterday's story left us with two questions:
1—How will Elijah go to heaven?
2—Will Elisha see him go?
Both are answered in today's reading...
**Read 2 Kings 2v11-15**

**TALK**

How did Elijah go to heaven? (v11) (*In a whirlwind.*) Did Elisha see him go? (v12) (*Yes*)

God gave Elisha **three signs** that he was to be God's prophet after Elijah:
**1—Elijah's cloak**. What happened to Elijah's cloak? (v13) (*Elisha picked it up and took it with him.*) This was a sign that he was carrying on the work of a prophet.
**2—Miracle**. What happened to the river Jordan? (v14) (*God parted it for Elisha to cross, just as He had for Elijah.*)
**3—The prophets**. What did the prophets say? (v15) (*That Elijah's spirit was resting on Elisha.*)

**THINK**

Do you ever think about **heaven**? <u>Everyone</u> who trusts in Jesus will one day live with Him in heaven. We don't know when or how we'll go, but we do know it will be **great**, because Jesus has promised to prepare a special place for us. (*That promise is in John 14v2.*) Talk to God about this now.

**PRAY**

### Building up
The prophets didn't really believe that Elijah had gone to heaven, so they sent out a search party! **Read 2 Kings 2v16-18** Did they find Elijah? (*No, because he really had gone.*)

# Extra Readings

## WHY ARE THERE EXTRA READINGS?

**Table Talk** and **XTB** both come out every three months. The main Bible reading pages contain material for 65 days. That's enough to use them Monday to Friday for three months.

Many families find that their routine is different at weekends from during the week. Some find that regular Bible reading fits in well on school days, but not at weekends. Others encourage their children to read the Bible for themselves during the week, then explore the Bible together as a family at weekends, when there's more time to do the activities together.

The important thing is to help your children get into the habit of reading the Bible for themselves—and that they see that regular Bible reading is important for **you** as well.

If you **are** able to read the Bible with your children every day, that's great! The extra readings on the next page will augment the main **Table Talk** pages so that you have enough material to cover the full three months.

You could:

- Read **Table Talk** every day for 65 days, then use the extra readings for the rest of the third month.

- Read **Table Talk** on weekdays. Use the extra readings at weekends.

- Use any other combination that works for your family.

## SOLOMON'S PROVERBS

As we saw on Day 17, God gave King Solomon the gift of *wisdom*. Solomon wrote the book of Proverbs to show us that loving and obeying God is the <u>wisest</u> way to live...

### Proverbs

*Proverbs are short sayings full of wisdom. They often tell us what <u>isn't</u> wise as well as what <u>is</u>.*

There are 26 Bible readings on the next three pages. Part of each verse has been printed for you—but with a word missing. Fill in the missing words as you read the verses. Then see if you can find them all in the wordsearch.

**Note:** Some are written backwards—or diagonally!!

| K | O | F | A | T | H | E | R | S | Y | T | G | X | D | N |
|---|---|---|---|---|---|---|---|---|---|---|---|---|---|---|
| G | N | S | R | E | H | T | O | M | Z | O | E | T | I | O |
| E | C | O | M | P | A | R | E | J | A | M | N | B | A | M |
| N | E | A | W | I | S | D | O | M | L | O | T | T | R | O |
| E | A | P | E | L | T | S | P | O | O | R | L | S | F | L |
| R | R | T | O | W | E | R | E | A | V | R | E | E | A | O |
| O | T | X | T | B | A | D | U | C | E | O | L | N | F | S |
| U | H | F | I | G | O | D | G | S | S | W | O | O | R | X |
| S | S | N | E | T | S | I | L | E | T | G | R | H | I | T |
| T | U | N | E | H | O | N | O | U | R | I | D | S | E | B |
| R | I | C | H | D | R | O | W | S | O | V | K | I | N | G |
| V | E | G | E | T | A | B | L | E | S | E | O | D | D | S |

# Extra Readings

## Chapter One

**1** ☐ **Read Proverbs 1v1-6**

*The book of Proverbs was written by King Solomon. He wrote Proverbs to give wisdom and understanding.*

'The proverbs of **S** _ _ _ _ _ _ son of David, the king of Israel.' (v1)

**2** ☐ **Read Proverbs 1v7**

*To 'fear' God doesn't mean being scared of Him! It means to love and respect God, and to show it by obeying Him. Solomon says that this is 'the beginning of knowledge'.*

'The fear of the LORD is the beginning of **k** _ _ _ _ _ _ _ _ _ .' (v7)

(Note: Some Bible versions say 'reverence' instead of 'fear'.)

**3** ☐ **Read Proverbs 1v8-9**

*Solomon tells us to listen to what our parents teach us, and not forget it!*

' Listen to your **f** _ _ _ _ _ _ ' teaching, and do not forget your **m** _ _ _ _ _ _ ' advice.' (v8)

**4** ☐ **Read Proverbs 1v10-19**

*Sometimes other people will try to get you to disobey God (to <u>sin</u>). Don't give in to them!*

'When sinners tempt you, do not **g** _ _ _ in to them.' (v10)

**5** ☐ **Read Proverbs 1v20-27**

*Solomon writes about 'wisdom' as if she is a person, calling out to people and warning them not to ignore her.*

' **W** _ _ _ _ _ _ calls aloud in the street, she raises her voice in the public squares.' (v20)

**6** ☐ **Read Proverbs 1v28-33**

*Solomon warns us of the dangers of ignoring 'wisdom', but then tells us that listening to 'wisdom' (and doing what she says) is the way to be safe, and not afraid.*

'Whoever **l** _ _ _ _ _ _ _ to me will be safe, with no reason to be afraid.' (v33)

## Chapter Three

**7** ☐ **Read Proverbs 3v1-4**

*If we are loving, kind and truthful, then we will please both God and other people.*

'Then you will be respected and pleasing to both **G** _ _ and men.' (v4)

**8** ☐ **Read Proverbs 3v5-6**

*God's ways are always best, so we should trust and obey Him—not just do what <u>we</u> think is best.*

'**T** _ _ _ _ _ in the LORD with all your heart. Don't depend on your own understanding.' (v5)

**9** ☐ **Read Proverbs 3v7-10**

*Solomon told the people to give God the best of what they owned. For them, that often meant the crops they grew. What could it be for you? (Your money? Your time? The things you're good at?).*

'**H** _ _ _ _ _ _ the LORD with your wealth.' (v9)

**10** ☐ **Read Proverbs 3v11-12**

*Parents who love their children don't ignore the wrong things they do. They correct them ('discipline' them) to help them change and grow up. God does the same thing.*

'The LORD disciplines (corrects) those He **l** _ _ _ _ .' (v12)

# Extra Readings

**11** ☐ **Read Proverbs 3v13-18**

*Living by God's wisdom is far better than having money and jewels!*

'Wisdom is more valuable than jewels; nothing you want could

c _ _ _ _ _ _ with her.' (v15)

**12** ☐ **Read Proverbs 3v19-20**

*God created our world, and everything in it, by His great wisdom.*

'The LORD created the e _ _ _ _ by His wisdom.' (v19)

**13** ☐ **Read Proverbs 3v21-26**

*Living God's way is <u>always</u> the best. If we do, we never need to be afraid.*

'You will not be a _ _ _ _ _ _ when you go to bed.' (v24)

**14** ☐ **Read Proverbs 3v27-35**

*If you're able to help someone, don't put it off, do it straight away.*

'Never tell your neighbour to wait until

t _ _ _ _ _ _ _ _ if you can help him now.' (v28)

## Living God's way

**15** ☐ **Read Proverbs 10v4-5**

*If you're lazy, you'll lose out.*

'Being l _ _ _ will make you poor.' (v4)

**16** ☐ **Read Proverbs 10v26**

*Don't be lazy. It's as irritating as drinking vinegar!!!*

'A lazy man will be as irritating as

v _ _ _ _ _ _ on your teeth or smoke in your eyes.' (v26)

**17** ☐ **Read Proverbs 11v1**

*God hates it when we cheat others.*

'The LORD hates d _ _ _ _ _ _ _ _ _ scales, but accurate weights are His delight.' (v1)

**18** ☐ **Read Proverbs 11v24-25**

*Giving things away <u>doesn't</u> mean we end up with nothing. Generous people are given much back.*

'Be g _ _ _ _ _ _ _ , and you will be prosperous. Help others, and you will be helped.' (v25)

**19** ☐ **Read Proverbs 12v17-19**

*Be careful how you use words, so that you help people rather than hurting them.*

'Thoughtless words can wound as deeply as any s _ _ _ _ but wisely spoken words can heal.' (v18)

**20** ☐ **Read Proverbs 15v1-2**

*If someone is angry with you, don't shout at them. Answer quietly and gently.*

'A g _ _ _ _ _ answer quietens anger, but a harsh one stirs it up.' (v1)

# Extra Readings

**21** ☐ **Read Proverbs 15v16-17**

*It's better to be with people you love, and who love God, even if they are poor, than to be with rich people who don't care about you.*

'Better to eat **v** _ _ _ _ _ _ _ _ _ with people you love than to eat the finest meat where there is hate.' (v17)

**22** ☐ **Read Proverbs 17v17**

*Being a good friend means loving and helping your friends at <u>all</u> times (good as well as bad). Who can you be a good friend to today?*

'A **f** _ _ _ _ _ loves at all times.' (v17)

## God is the Real King

**23** ☐ **Read Proverbs 18v10**

*God is like a strong tower. If we trust in Him, He will keep us safe.*

'The name of the LORD is a strong **t** _ _ _ _ .' (v10)

# WHAT NEXT?

We hope that **Table Talk** has helped you get into a regular habit of reading the Bible with your children.

**Table Talk** comes out every three months. Each issue contains 65 full **Table Talk** outlines, plus 26 days of extra readings. By the time you've used them all, the next issue will be available.

Available from your local Christian bookshop—or call us on **0845 225 0880** to order a copy.

**24** ☐ **Read Proverbs 19v21**

*God is the Real King. His plans <u>always</u> work out.*

'People may plan all kinds of things, but the **L** _ _ _ **'s** will is going to be done.' (v21)

**25** ☐ **Read Proverbs 21v1-3**

*Kings and Presidents might seem powerful—but it's <u>God</u> who's really in control!*

'The LORD controls the mind (heart) of a **k** _ _ _ as easily as He directs the course of a stream.' (v1)

**26** ☐ **Read Proverbs 22v2**

*God made all of us. He is our Maker, our loving Father and our King.*

'The **r** _ _ _ and the **p** _ _ _ have this in common: the LORD is the Maker of them all.' (v2)

## COMING SOON!
### Issue Eleven of Table Talk

Issue Eleven of Table Talk explores the books of John, 2 Kings, Isaiah and Jeremiah.

- The Gospel of **John** tells us all about Jesus. Read about some more of the miracles that pointed to <u>who</u> Jesus is.
- Meet Elisha, and some of the kings of Israel and Judah in the book of **2 Kings**.
- Meet the prophets **Isaiah** and **Jeremiah**, and hear their messages for God's people.